Talk Matters

REFOCUSING THE LANGUAGE
OF PUBLIC SCHOOLING

Talk Matters

REFOCUSING THE LANGUAGE OF PUBLIC SCHOOLING

Beatrice S. Fennimore

Foreword by James W. Fraser

Teachers College, Columbia University
New York and London

Published by Teachers College Press, 1234 Amsterdam Avenue, New York, NY 10027

Library of Congress Cataloging-in-Publication Data

Fennimore, Beatrice Schneller.
    Talk matters : refocusing the language of public schooling / Beatrice S. Fennimore; foreword by James W. Fraser.
        p.   cm.
    Includes bibliographical references (p.   ) and index.
        ISBN 0-8077-3903-0 (cloth : alk. paper) — ISBN 0-8077-3902-2 (pbk. : alk. paper)
        1. Communication in education.   2. Public schools—Social aspects—United States.   3. Sociolinguistics—United States.   I. Title.
    LB1033.5F46   2000
    370′.1′4—dc21   99-047225

ISBN 0-8077-3902-2 (paper)
ISBN 0-8077-3903-0 (cloth)

Printed on acid-free paper
Manufactured in the United States of America

07 06 05 04 03 02 01 00   8 7 6 5 4 3 2 1

To Mrs. Mary Ann Fennimore, whose life has spoken a
language of great love for children everywhere

Contents

Foreword

Three decades ago, when the struggle for quality desegregated education was just beginning in the Boston Public Schools, one of the old line conservatives on the Boston School Committee complained about the protesters who were demanding reform, by saying, "There is nothing wrong with the Boston Public Schools. The problem is the quality of kids these parents are sending us." Over the intervening decades, many in the field of education have become more sophisticated in their language. But the comment continues to frame far too much of the conversation. One of the unfortunate by-products of the extraordinary efforts of the federal government to improve the educational opportunities for all of the nation's children during the reforms of the Great Society era was the development of a new literature and a new language for "understanding" why some children did not perform as well as others. The result was an alphabet soup of deficits from "special needs," to "non-English speaking," to "at risk," to the omnipresent "minority," all of which tend to denigrate the students and, if not directly blaming the students—after all, it is not the student's fault that all of the negatives have piled up—still absolving the school systems and the teachers of significant responsibility for bringing about change. The result is the development of a widely accepted educational language that directly impedes the fundamental role of schooling in a democratic society—providing the best possible education for every child, linked to the high expectation that every child will prosper when offered such opportunity.

In TALK MATTERS, Beatrice Fennimore has offered us a very important tool for challenging and changing this sad state of affairs. Fennimore begins with the simple assertion that how we talk about kids matters. Who can disagree? We educators cannot go through our days talking about the low potential and low achievement of our students and not have it impact our work. As Fennimore shows so clearly, for all of the reform efforts, the language of the profession remains a language of damage and deficit, which results in "widespread public stereotyping of all students who live in areas associated with poverty." And anyone who spends too much time talking about the problems of "single-parent children, poor children, children who did not begin life speaking English, etc. etc.," will—no matter what the initial good intentions—come to view these children as also having limited potential. The result is a self-fulfilling prophecy in which low expectations lead to low achievements, which leads to lower expectations and lower achievement, and no one is seen as at fault—after all, the problems came to the school with the children.

It is not only teachers and citizens at large who pick up on the deficit language. Children know how adults view them, and the adult expectations become their expectations. Many years ago I began my own educational career as a fourth-grade teacher in a rigidly tracked public school in New York City. The fourth-grade classes in this large school were ranked, but there was an ever-changing color code for which class was best and which worst. Although teachers occasionally forgot if the greens were better readers than the purples or vice versa, the students never forgot. They knew the code, they referred to it, and they reminded the teachers.

Professor Fennimore offers more than critique of this situation, although she does that most effectively. She also goes on to talk about what meaningful change might sound like. She describes real-world examples of teachers who have transcended the "I don't know how they can expect us to deal with impaired kids . . . " mentality and who have moved on to "This situation has helped me to become a better teacher." In proposing an ethical code for educators, Fennimore begins with the question that could change everything: "If I were a parent of children in this school, how might I respond to the conversations that take place in the classrooms, hallways, the teachers' lounge, and faculty meetings?" This may be the early-twenty-first-century version of John Dewey's early-twentieth-century question—whether schools could offer every child "what the best and wisest parent wants for his or her child." And the question is as essential as ever.

Fennimore is clear that the solution for these issues will not be easy. Harried teachers and administrators have many things about which to be concerned. Including their own language on the list is not going to be popular. But, as this volume shows so well, change is both possible and necessary. I hope that many, many teachers and future teachers, school leaders, and parents will read TALK MATTERS and demand the kinds of changes called for here—beginning with themselves. The result can be a whole new way of viewing the wonderful potential of the young citizens who inhabit our schools today and who will share this nation with us and inherit it from us in the future. For all of the problems described here, this is a deeply optimistic volume. If we can all take it with sufficient seriousness, the schooling offered America's youth in the twenty-first century will be fundamentally different and better than that of the past.

James W. Fraser
Northeastern University

Preface

This is the low group.

Most of our kids come from homes that don't value education.

The majority of our students are SED, LD, or ADHD.

Half of the kindergarten students were crack babies.

Our students tend to be poor, which leads to lower test scores.

Our kind of kid tends to walk past junkies to get to school.

How should responsible educators think about statements like those above? Are the speakers "just talking" among themselves, without ramification for the children being discussed? Or, do these deficit-based statements have a powerful effect on the ultimate educational outcomes of students laboring under such ponderous descriptions? In answering these questions, educators on all levels are challenged to examine the ethical and moral dimensions of the language used to discuss and describe students in a democratic society.

I have written this book to develop a conceptualization of educational language as a *professional behavior* that has significant effects on student outcomes in educational institutions. Within that context, educational language is defined as the way in which educators discuss, describe, categorize, and verbally expect behaviors and achievements from students in educational institutions as well as in the process of scholarship and research. The patterns of educational language in any educational institution or endeavor create the *language environment*, also known as the semantic environment, which embodies the totality of what is said, how it is said, why it is said, and the overt and covert effects of saying it. When language is viewed as an *action* or a *behavior*, its moral, ethical, and professional ramifications become clear. Educators are never "just talking" when they speak about students either in institutional settings or in the public arena. The linguistic representation of children on any level of the educational endeavor constructs reality for those children, and for the professionals who are responsible to them. I argue in this book that the action of language constantly moves from description into determinism, and thus that events and outcomes are determined through speech. Ultimately, language represents the social, political, and cultural power embodied in all educational institutions.

As a teacher educator at a large state university, who has done extensive field supervision in many urban, rural, and suburban schools, I have a long-standing concern about educational language. How, I have wondered for years, might a solution be found to the seemingly intractable problem of deficit-based terminology and dismissive language about children whose race, socioeconomic status, or ethnic characteristics are stereotypically associated with low expectations for academic and personal performance? While I have continued to embrace the power of multicultural education to change attitudes underlying negative language, the persistent presence of deficit terminology seems also to require a more focused approach. Thus, I decided to integrate my commitments to multiculturalism, child advocacy, and public school equity into an examination of the moral and ethical dimensions of language in and of itself.

In Chapter 1, I introduce the conceptualization of language as a critical, and potentially transformative, educational behavior. Chapter 2 then develops the relationship of educational language to the challenge of democracy and explores the ways in which language can open possibilities when it is characterized by social responsibility, morality, and inquiry. In Chapter 3, I move into a closer examination of the relationship of language to educational institutions, with a particular focus on the mandate of public education and the persistent challenge of student classification. Chapter 4 extends the discussion of language into the wider arena of school restructuring and reform, and the ways in which language affects professional collaboration. In Chapter 5, I examine the historical bonds of deficit terminology, which have influenced and continue to permeate educational language. Then, Chapter 6 establishes the role of educational leadership, policy, and teacher education in altering the historical negative patterns of language. Chapter 7 moves into a discussion of language and the everyday in schools, and develops a conceptualization of ethical codes as an approach to intractable institutional language dilemmas. Finally, Chapter 8 examines the way in which a school might analyze its own language environment and develop an ethical code focused on deficit terminology, student classification and tracking, and confidential information about students.

In the hope of making my ideas as useful as possible to the reader, I have incorporated examples of situational uses of language throughout this book. Also, I have created activities at the end of every chapter that enhance understanding of basic concepts. Finally, in Chapter 8, I include an example of an ethical code of language to be utilized in a school setting. This code is adaptable to any setting in which a reader might want to undertake examination and improvement of the educational language environment.

Acknowledgments

My greatest thanks are due to Susan Liddicoat, my editor and friend at Teachers College Press, without whom this book could not have been written. From our preliminary conversations about this project many years ago, and through a seemingly endless series of interruptions and delays, Susan's extraordinary patience and understanding have been combined with unswerving support. Her excellent editing and consistently fine advice have vastly improved every aspect of the final manuscript. I am grateful also to the late Ron Galbraith, and to Sarah Biondello, for their support and advice on my earlier ideas about this book. Robert Nash was very generous in his review of this manuscript, as he extended excellent, detailed ideas combined with enthusiastic encouragement. His chapter-by-chapter suggestions for revisions were enormously useful and added a great deal to the quality of the final manuscript. Finally, heartfelt gratitude to Jim Fraser, who graciously took time from his demanding schedule to read this manuscript and write the Foreword. I am honored by his contribution.

Marvin Fein has been not only a wonderful and supportive partner, but a keen editor as well. He read the entire manuscript and, utilizing his expertise in analytic writing, helped me to fine-tune and clarify many important points throughout. My daughters Sharon and Maryann have inspired me with their many insightful reflections into their own past public school experiences, and their sensitivity to the continuing need for equal educational opportunities for all children. Maryann, a senior at the Rhode Island School of Design, delighted me by offering to illustrate the cover of this book.

I want to thank all of my students, who continue to be my best teachers, and to express appreciation to colleagues who have given support and encouragement. Indiana University of Pennsylvania provided the sabbatical that made it possible for me to research and develop the first draft of this book. I am indebted to the many children whose schools I have been fortunate enough to visit in the course of my work. My growing awareness of the ways in which their human dignity and boundless potential could be placed at risk by negative labels, deficit terminology, and biased expectations, became the foundation of my commitment to ethical educational language.

On the day I decided that I wanted to dedicate this book to someone whose positive and caring words about children made a tremendous difference in the world, my mind turned immediately to my daughters' warm and loving grandmother, Mrs. Mary Ann Fennimore. To me, Mary Ann symbolizes the quiet, persistent, powerful contributions made by women who extend a lifetime of care, not only to their own children and grandchildren, but to many others in their family and community. As the oldest daughter in a large extended family in Brooklyn, Mary Ann was responsible at a young age for taking care of many younger children whose parents were in need of help. Her divorced mother who worked long hours as a seamstress, her pregnant aunt who was widowed with two small boys at home, her aunt and uncle with tiny twins, her sickly aunt with a rambunctious son, her aunt with two young daughters who suddenly lost her husband in a Brooklyn Union Gas Company explosion— these and many others depended on her faithful assistance. Even on the night of her own wedding, Mary Ann, the 20-year-old bride, could not leave for her honeymoon before kissing and comforting the children who were going to miss her back at home. When her husband Joseph returned from active duty in Germany during World War II, they raised five children together. Mary Ann's love for and loyalty to her children, and ultimately to her grandchildren, is legend. She has exemplified heartfelt dedication to her family, as well as concern about each and every child who has crossed her path, throughout her life. And through all the heavy responsibilities she has carried from early adolescence to her later years, Mary Ann's words have always embodied hope and encouragement for all around her.

Talk Matters

REFOCUSING THE LANGUAGE
OF PUBLIC SCHOOLING

1

We're Not Just Talking: Taking a New Look at Educational Language

Educators are faced today with massive change and reform in schools all over America. Certainly the movement to restructure and improve education is positive and promising. A balance must be achieved, however, between futuristic planning and a commitment to meet the current needs of children in our schools. In a shifting educational and social climate, it is dangerously easy to lose sight of our critical responsibility to the children whose only chance to receive an education is taking place right now. Some projected school reforms, although very promising, are going to require extensive time and greater resources for full implementation. In the present climate of federal and state cost cutting, a time line for many proposed reforms is uncertain. Therefore, I believe that it is important for educators to also envision reforms that can be implemented with some sense of immediacy. One such reform, which would have deep and far-reaching effects, would be *a deliberate change in the ways educators talk about categorizations and expectations in educational environments*. In other words, the customarily used professional language of educators could be recreated to open doors for more productive ways of thinking and talking about children.

THE CHALLENGE OF EDUCATIONAL LANGUAGE

Educational language can be viewed as a semantic environment. Postman and Weingartner (1969) define a semantic environment as any human situation in which language plays a critical role. They describe the constituents of a semantic environment as (1) people, (2) their purposes, and (3) the language

1

they use to achieve their purposes. I will refer to the *educational language environment* rather than the semantic environment and will define the educational language environment as the totality of *what is said, how it is said, why it is said, and the intended and unintended efforts of saying it.* Furthermore, I will assume that educational language environments exist in many related contexts, including schools (early childhood programs, elementary, middle, and high schools), colleges and universities, school boards and their proceedings, educational organizations, and professional teachers' unions. The talking of educators or those whose work is connected to education in each of the above contexts has significant ramifications for all in the profession—and all the children the profession is designed to serve.

Looking at Educational Language from the Outside-in

How do noneducators perceive the habitual ways in which those who work in the field of education talk about students in American schools? It might be interesting to step away from one's familiar educational environment and conceptualize the way it would be viewed in the eyes of others. Imagine, for instance, that as a citizen but not an educator, you have decided out of pure interest to attend a large national conference of a prestigious educational organization. You might be a parent concerned about future educational choices for your children, or a businessperson interested in investment in educational initiatives. In any case, you attend many conference sessions, panels, and presentations to develop more insight into the theme of school restructuring. The first thing you notice is a great deal of exciting discussion about school reform and futuristic ideas about educational innovations and possibilities. Professional educators from a wide variety of institutions are describing ways in which schools can be more attuned to the needs and interests of teachers, administrators, children, families, and communities. You are developing the welcome impression that American education is at a point of positive and productive change. However, as you continue to listen closely to the many educational conversations around you, a troubling and discordant note begins to emerge. While educational progress is being discussed in positive terms, a significant number of American students seem continuously to be described with negative terminology. Your otherwise positive response to conference themes becomes clouded by a steadily emerging picture of children who are needy, deficient, below the norm, or developmentally delayed. You begin to listen more closely to what is said about students:

Since the majority of our children are on public assistance or qualify for free lunch, it is not surprising that our test scores are well below the national norm.

Our students are the kinds of kids who walk to school past gangs and crack houses.

This district serves a majority of children who enter school with low IQ scores predictive of low academic achievement throughout the early grades.

This kind of creative curriculum might work well in wealthier areas, but our urban population tends to be of low academic ability. It would be useless to attempt this in our district.

Almost 45% of our students qualify for Title I services, which should give you insight into the serious nature of their ongoing academic problems.

As you continue to attend sessions, you repeatedly hear about low IQ scores, lack of readiness to enter kindergarten, lack of parental concern, pervasive poverty, trauma created by violence in homes and communities, and declining test scores throughout the country. After just a few days at the conference, you become familiar with consistently used terminology:

crack babies
developmentally delayed
learning disabled
low standardized test scores
achievement gaps
socially and emotionally disturbed
at risk
disadvantaged

Several speakers have added to your growing sense of discouragement by referring to the possibility of permanent damage to cognitive growth caused by early poverty. Others have identified brain or behavioral dysfunction associated with exposure to alcohol or drugs in vitro. The seeming hopelessness of these possibilities saddens you. The longer you remain at the conference, the more you wonder if any of the innovations or reforms under discussion are relevant or realistic in the depressing context of what you are hearing about school students. How *can* the schools move ahead under this shadow of low IQ scores, lack of readiness for school, lack of parental concern, pervasive poverty, emotional and physical trauma created by violence in homes and communities, and declining test scores throughout America?

If you had been a parent at this conference, you might well have decided to avoid public schools, or urban public schools, or schools that any of the children you have heard so negatively described are likely to attend. Perhaps you might come to believe that parents of well-functioning children can only select more elite environments so their children are not dragged down by all those who are falling behind. If you were a businessperson at this conference, you might re-evaluate the ways in which you want to invest in educational initiatives. Knowing that innovative projects often are judged by outcomes in terms of standardized test scores, you might decide to avoid becoming involved with schools serving less-advantaged children, who tend to do less well on such assessments.

As a noneducator participant at the conference, you come away with a new awareness of the ways in which children are stratified in school and society. You are also more aware of the existence of both visionary educators as well as educators whose vision seems clouded by negativity toward children. You feel less confident in the future of the schools and now question the professional commitments of some education professionals.

The Importance of Educational Language

The imagined citizen at the educational conference was deeply affected by descriptive language about students. Educators construct the public perception of school students in important ways. Public confidence in public schools, and in current efforts aimed toward reform, can be undermined by the negative talk of professionals. Furthermore, educators who habitually discuss their students as inherently unequal in potential and ability may undermine public interest in or support of equity initiatives. This period of reform brings with it the urgent need for educators to reflect on and re-evaluate their public use of language about schools and students. I have found that the tremendous energy put into educational reform has not effectively altered old and entrenched patterns of deficit-based descriptions of children. These descriptions, often reinforced by institutional habits of labeling and stratification, can create significant barriers to any substantial gains for children that might be generated by school reform.

Although educators should be aware of public perceptions they create about American children, their greatest concern should be the ways in which their use of descriptive language *actually shapes the school experiences and educational outcomes of students.* Educators never "just talk." The language environment of any school or other educational institution serves as a dynamic platform for powerful attitudes and behaviors. The habit of routinely describing students as deficient, or at risk, or delayed, poses an unacceptable danger to their development. The language of educational deficiency is neither neutral nor benign; the assignment of negative value has serious repercussions for the child. The educational language environment permeates many levels of human belief and behavior in the educational institution. Educators, like all people, tend to habitually divide their daily experiences into linguistic categories. Once these categories are well established in the human psyche, all new perceptions tend to be organized into them. If the habitual linguistic categories available to educators focus on disability, deficit, and the prediction of failure, then those very categories continually can prejudice thoughts and actions in educational institutions (Postman & Weingartner, 1969).

Students invariably sense the attitudes and feelings of professionals who routinely describe them in terms of deficiency. They also experience serious repercussions from constant public dialogue about their presumed educational or familial inadequacies. Indiscriminate and constant public disclosure of children's weaknesses or personal problems can intensify damaging effects in their social environments and reinforce unfortunate discriminatory beliefs about them within the general public. If most of the children of America were thriving, and thus only a small percentage were in danger of attracting negative educational descriptors, the issue of educational language might be less urgent (although no less important). In fact, however, an unprecedented number of American children are experiencing current disadvantage and stress. These difficulties play a central role in the ways in which educational language can and should be reconstructed.

THE CHALLENGE OF CHILDHOOD IN AMERICA

The entire issue of educational language, most particularly deficit-based educational language, is intricately complicated by current challenges to the safe and healthy development of many children in the United States. The Council on Families in America (Steinfels, 1992) stated that the current generation of children and youth is the first in the nation to be less well off psychologically, socially, economically, and morally than their parents were at the same age. The daunting evidence cited by the council included the fact that a fifth of the nation's children were poor, as were almost a fourth of its preschoolers and half of its African American children. One in four children was born to an unmarried mother, reports of child neglect and abuse increased by 40%, juvenile crime more than doubled, and rates of teen-age suicide and death by homicide more than tripled.

In a similar vein, the final report of the National Commission on Children (1991) stated that children were the poorest Americans, with more than 2 million more children living in poverty than a decade ago. Nearly 5 million

children were desperately poor, with family incomes of less than half the federal
poverty level. More than 8 million children were numbered among the 32
million Americans who had no form of health insurance coverage. The growing
epidemic of alcohol and illegal drug use, especially the use of crack cocaine,
by pregnant women severely threatened the health and development of as
many as 375,000 babies a year. One in five children in America between the
ages of 3 and 17 was reported by parents to have a developmental delay,
learning disability, or behavioral problem. Children from single-parent families
were two to three times as likely to suffer such problems as children living
with both parents.

While facts and figures shift somewhat from year to year, these concerns
continue to be prominent and worrisome. Taylor (1996) cites an estimate that
close to one-third of Americans fall into poverty by age 15 and that half of
American children live in near-poverty at some time during childhood. Taylor
also states that among eight industrialized countries, the United States has the
highest rate of single-parent families and that the U.S. rates of teen pregnancy
and birth are highest among six industrialized countries. The Children's Defense
Fund (1995) reports that between 3.3 million and 10 million children are
exposed to domestic violence each year and that an estimated 7.7 million
children in the United States suffer from serious emotional disorders. The
same report indicates that guns killed 5,379 children and teens in 1992.

Although these and other distressing indications about the current welfare
children have been relatively well-known for some time, they have not yet met
with a concerted public willingness to alleviate the problems. In fact, the final
report of the National Commission on Children (1991) indicated that the
profound changes in child and family life over the past generation were unlikely
to be reversed for some time. Americans have not had an easy time comprehend-
ing these changes or deciding how to adapt to them. Children have continued
to pay the price for the slow response of public- and private-sector policies
and programs, community institutions, and families themselves.

In fact, rather than using available information about children to foster
greater social support, Americans currently are experiencing what Stephen
Jay Gould (as quoted in Banks, 1995a) identified as "a historical moment of
unprecedented ungenerosity" (p. 22). Major societal sentiments of the times
include calls for closing the nation's borders to foreigners and radical reform
of welfare and other programs targeted for low-income groups (Banks, 1995a).
With the passage of the Personal Responsibility and Work Opportunity Act of
1996, the American government ended 6 decades of entitlement to the poor.
While state implementation of that legislation is not yet complete, the possibility
exists that poverty among American children will increase. The continuation
of current social and economic trends indicates that all who educate must

be prepared to meet the considerable needs of a stressed American child population.

Honesty and Vision as Advocacy

All Americans, particularly those whose professions are closely aligned to children and families, should be disturbed by the presence of such dire needs in our rich nation. I believe that educators, who must strive to function competently in spite of so many challenges, must make an ethical choice regarding how they will describe and talk about the problems of their students. On one the hand, it is their right and responsibility to be *honest* about the ways in which poverty, violence, neglect, and family disintegration interfere with the optimal development of their students. On the other hand, they must still be accountable for *provision of excellent educational opportunities* for all children. Rather than using the current situation as an excuse for educational failures (although desperate circumstances outside the school undoubtedly contribute to failures), educators must continue to articulate the determined intention to create school environments that provide children with optimal opportunities for growth and success. To do any less would be to fall seriously short of the ethics and ideals of educational professionalism. Furthermore, it would be difficult to justify the continued existence of public schools if the educators within them did not believe that their students could be educated successfully.

How might a balance be achieved between honest acknowledgment of children's problems and a determined vision of their present and future possibilities? It would be morally wrong to attempt to silence educators or pressure them to censure the truth about the many challenges and dilemmas confronting their students. In fact, the truth can place educators in an excellent position to be *advocates* who use their knowledge and experience to build political support for improved child and family policies. Nothing can be gained from hiding the truth, and much could be gained if the statement of the truth generated greater social concern.

Meaningful reconstruction of educational language, then, would be far removed from any attempt to build better public relations between schools and society through manipulation of information about children. The focus rather would be on the *construction of a positive and visionary perspective* of what is true but also of what might be possible if children received excellent opportunities. The challenge to construct better uses of educational language is not necessarily situated in specific information about children that is relayed to other educators and to the public. The challenge is more closely related to this question: Is the information couched in terms of respect for children and responsibility to do all that is possible for them, or is it couched in terms of a

sense of hopelessness and a lack of professional accountability? *How* are challenges or deficiencies explained and described, *why* are some children rather
than others consistently engulfed in an impersonal cloud of negativity (such as
children who are poor), and *what happens* when deficit-based descriptions
carry unfair generalities that lead to the assumption of inferiority and school
failure? It is these questions that can guide the reconstruction of educational
language.

Compounding Children's Problems

There are three particularly worrisome problems inherent in current educational talk about children. One concern arises when educators habitually use
deficit-based terminology without questioning its basic assumptions or ultimate
outcomes. What does it really mean, for example, to say that most of the
students in a certain school are at risk? Is there any positive outcome associated
with such a statement, or will it simply reinforce negative or hopeless attitudes
already in place?

A second concern is the well-documented tendency for deficit-based descriptions to be attached to children from economically, racially, culturally,
and linguistically diverse backgrounds. These negative descriptions tend to
be related to parallel tracking or grouping designations that limit access to
opportunities.

The third concern is related to the question of ethics and client (the child
and family) confidentiality that arises when personal sufferings or shortcomings
are discussed publicly by educators. How can schoolchildren be protected from
the vulnerability created by the access of a large number of educators to deeply
sensitive information about their lives? How do educators collect and articulate
data concerning the private lives of children and families? With whom is
sensitive data shared, and for what purpose?

Educators who reconstruct their language must give attention to the possibility that deficit-based language often reflects discrimination and harmful
stereotyping, that confidentiality is betrayed when indiscriminate sharing of
sensitive personal information about clients occurs, and that negative educational talk can compound existing problems rather than provide humane forms
of relief. Without attention to the above areas of concern, educators are continually at risk for the betrayal of their own primary mission by compounding the
problems of children. But as educators reconstruct their language, they also
deserve full understanding of the problems and difficulties they experience as
they work hard to serve their students. Therefore, before further discussing
reconstruction of educational language, it is important to examine the problems
faced by the current generation of American teachers.

THE CHALLENGE OF TEACHING IN AMERICA

The problems of children and their teachers are intricately connected. Teaching is a deeply personal endeavor. Personal involvement in the lives of children who are experiencing sadness or serious difficulty places considerable stress on teachers. Troubled by barriers to the success of their students outside the school, which may well be compounded by a lack of resources and opportunities inside the school, some teachers cannot help but wonder if their skills might better be used in a less depressing environment. It can be so frustrating for them to sense the limitations of their efforts and caring for their students. It can be so hard to know that so many children are consumed with fear, hunger, untreated physical or emotional problems, family tragedy, or abuse and neglect. Furthermore, the teachers who willingly embrace their challenges are still routinely included in general public criticism of teachers and schools. Educators have the right to resent unfair blame for circumstances outside the school that indeed detract from their intensive and dedicated efforts. It is truly a moral challenge for them to resist a temptation to vent their frustration through negative talk about students, families, and communities. No one should take that challenge lightly, or point a finger at teachers without considering the difficulties inherent in all they willingly undertake.

It is not only the general public, but also educational scholars or researchers not directly connected with the daily life of classrooms, who should be careful not to overlook the debilitating effects of constant frustrations on some teachers. The constant influx of new students, difficulty in maintaining dialogue with stressed and busy families, lack of adequate resources such as paper and books, and lack of adequate support services for students would be potentially discouraging to anyone. One classroom teacher, Susan Ohanian (1988), openly wondered how many commission members or community leaders were familiar with the debilitating effects of daily interruptions and inconveniences in the classroom. Many teachers, she wrote, "would cheerfully give up their copies of the reports on excellence for a ream of paper, a handful of #2 pencils, or a box of staples that fit the stapler" (p. 317).

Teachers, not unlike many of their students, demonstrate a rather remarkable resilience by facing the daily challenge of life in classrooms. Every potential educational reformer should acknowledge and care about the feelings and frustrations of classroom teachers. Failure to do so, or scapegoating teachers for problems beyond their control, creates an unfortunate climate in which overwhelmed teachers might focus their own frustrations on the limitations of children, families, and communities. The best way to avoid the above dilemmas is to move all discussion of educational reform, including the need to reconstruct the language of education, well beyond the scope of directives for classroom teachers. Everyone whose professional work is connected to education and public schooling in any capacity should be equally involved in the reconstruction of educational language—a reconstruction as sensitive to teachers as it is to the American child population.

RECOGNIZING THE POWER OF WORDS

Rhees (1963) wrote that words always connect what people are saying and doing; what we say makes a difference and the expressions we use make a difference. The prior discussion of the serious problems of children, for example, quite possibly could be discouraging to some readers. Many who ponder the sobering realities about American children are tempted at least at times to ask: Is there really *anything* that can be done to make a difference at this point? Consider the statement of Chester Finn, quoted in *The New York Times* (Applebome, 1997), that, even with perfect school attendance, children spend only 9% of their time from birth to age 18 in school. How, he asks, could 9% possibly make up for the other 91%? How, indeed! This is the very challenge that must be embraced by all educators. Schooling enhances the growth of the hearts and minds of children, and children use their hearts and minds every minute of their lives. Positive growth in school thus can change everything, hard as that might be to observe and measure in the short term.

The challenge is to struggle against the odds to locate significant points of power that open windows of hope and opportunity. Reconstructed educational language has considerable power, not only to protect idealistic and visionary efforts of educators but to help educators support the growth of a greater commitment in the general public to excellent and equitable public schools for all children.

Conceptualizing Educational Language Environments

How might one begin to conceptualize the language environment of an educational setting? A good way to begin would be envisioning what might occur during the careful observation of the use of professional language within a given school. For example, imagine that a group of visitors are spending a day in the public school of an economically stressed community to observe the ways in which children are described. What might these visitors learn about attitudes, beliefs, and opportunities for children simply by listening to what is said about them? What discussions and descriptions might they hear or overhear?

One possibility is that the existing stratification of students would become almost immediately apparent ("Of course we do have some advanced students, but the majority are falling way behind"). Also quickly apparent might be the fact that the existing stratification matters very much in the ways children are treated within the school ("We have to maintain a lot of control over these slower children, so they stay in their classrooms during most assemblies"). The visitors might quickly develop the strong sense that they would want their own children to receive one school designation ("This is the brightest group") over others ("You'll note these children seem to be struggling; this is our transitional kindergarten/first grade"). As the observation continues, the visitors might develop a growing concern about some of the attitudes inherent in the professional talk about children ("Many of these children will never make it through high school . . . some of the students will never be able to catch up . . . the parents are totally unconcerned about education"). By the end of the visit, observation and subsequent analysis of the language environment would possibly have indicated many areas of negativity and discouragement. The talk of teachers and administrators had revealed a wide span of professional attitudes and expectations—some far more positive and hopeful than others. Likewise, the educational talk indicated a wide variety of experiences for children within the school, some more attractive and interesting than others.

Now reconsider the same scenario from a different perspective. Imagine the visitors entering a school that almost immediately exudes an overall respect for the potential of all students—although it also is quickly clear that some students are more advanced than others at that point in time. They might hear about real problems ("Sad to say, many of our students are deeply affected by violence in home or community . . . much as we wish it otherwise, many of our children have not yet reached national reading norms"). However, these truthful disclosures routinely are not connected to parallel school stratification of obvious differences in the attitudes and expectations of educators. A first-grade group might be described in the following way:

> Take a look at the independent activities being done in this classroom. Some of the children currently have a special education designation, or are receiving special therapy to relieve problems associated with exposure to drugs in vitro. Others have experienced much less difficulty in school, and some of them are quite advanced in terms of academics. We learn so much about the strengths of all these children from assessment of their independent projects.

From the above description, the visitors know that children are diverse in terms of experience and current ability. However, they cannot tell which children have received different designations because the language used does not reveal personal identity or reflect an entrenched system of stratification. They have a positive impression of the school because of their sense that all the children, regardless of current status, are receiving a fair chance to succeed. They have identified an *overall climate of high expectation*, which has not allowed the problems of students to interfere with perception of their potential.

   The Connection of Stratification to Language. The preceding example shows that educational language is closely related to school practice. When schools label and track students, the resulting stratification is very likely to be evident in the language environment. I want to maintain focus, however, on *language itself.* Whatever the institutional practices may be, and there are indeed many schools in which stratification related to tracking and grouping is highly visible, educational talk is still a separate entity. Whatever the circumstances, there continue to be many choices in the description of student ability. A child may be described as "slow" or "retarded" in contrast to "currently falling behind some of the norms we expect at this age." Educators working with children experiencing some developmental delays may say, "Evidence exists that they will never catch up," or more positively, "We continually seek to assess and hope for student gains." What educators say, and how they say it, makes a very big difference in all aspects of schooling.

   Considering all the social and economic barriers to high student performance, is it naive to propose that the language environment makes a critical difference? It is not, as long as two central educational commitments continue to be embraced:

1. The belief that educators have an ethical responsibility to seek the most positive avenues for the optimal development of every child. This means that educators do not have the right, no matter how stressed they may be, to denigrate or give up on children.
2. The belief that idealistic principles of a democratic society should be adopted by all educators who serve American children. This means that the principles of *equality and liberty,* so revered in the American Constitution, should support efforts of educators to protect the rights of every student to dignity and access to full development of personal potential.

These two central commitments are the fundamental structure on which educators can build expansive improvements in all aspects of education. An essential component of this structure is the continual construction of an educational language environment that supports the inherent freedom of children to grow and change throughout their schooling.

   Ideals sometimes can be clouded by shocking realities in children's lives. Homelessness, violent abuse, severe malnourishment—these and many other problems really do hamper the ability of children to do well in school. Even for children facing issues such as these, however, a positive educational language environment protects and supports a vision of a better future. Passow and Elliott (1968) emphasized the role of public schools in rescuing children from hopelessness by opening continual avenues of unexplored opportunity. This role, they wrote, is beyond dispute; it is the life's work of educational institutions and all who serve children within them. Positive educational language is the critical first step in creating an environment of hope within the school. Describing each child as equally worthy of exposure to excellent opportunities sets the stage for the continual provision of a full and meaningful education.

Analyzing Professional Literature. Since the civil rights movement of the 1960s, a great deal of national attention has focused on issues of poverty in America. The needs of children who are economically disadvantaged have been the focus of a great deal of research and publication in social and behavioral sciences as well as in education. But describing children in professional literature in negative terms can undermine the potential success of subsequent efforts to help them. Once any group of people is perceived by the public as generally deficient or incompetent, negative social ramifications are almost impossible to avoid.

To further consider the seriousness of this problem, reflect on this description of low-income neighborhoods:

> The conditions common to low-income neighborhoods and their school children . . . untreated serious health problems, developmental disabilities, hunger, neighborhood violence, more family disruption, lower parent education and participation, and frequent moving to escape threatening conditions . . . often overwhelm efforts for effective schooling. (Orfield & Eaton, 1996, p. 83)

The content of this statement is not uncommon to descriptions of communities experiencing poverty conditions. These authors, not unlike many authors in the social sciences, supply this information to strengthen the argument for a need for social intervention (school desegregation, in this case). The *problem* with such descriptions, although they are written with a desire to advocate for children, is that the generalizations contained in them could reinforce widespread public stereotyping of *all* students who live in areas associated with poverty. The picture can appear so hopeless that the public becomes resistant to continued social and economic interventions for seemingly intractable problems. Likewise, some families and educators will fear association with schools attended by children who are poor. If teacher education also is permeated with generalized images of children in poor economic circumstances, even the teachers who choose to teach in schools where poverty is pervasive, may approach their work with the deep-seated belief that the children really cannot learn successfully.

Now, it might be argued that the above description is truthful and that the public should be aware of the conditions of low-income neighborhoods. However, the truth varies from individual to individual and community to community. No one would really suggest that *every* child in a low-income neighborhood has the same problems and characteristics, or that *every* family in a low-income neighborhood is dysfunctional. From the perspectives of the children, families, and communities described, a variety of other perspectives undoubtedly wound emerge. Perhaps the authors who routinely cite negative information, albeit to help those with undeniable problems, need to find ways to express the facts in a more open context of hope. (*Some* children are highly resilient, *some* families are strong and resourceful in the worst of circumstances, and *some* schools in low-income communities exhibit remarkable progress with students.) While the pressing argument of the work might be somewhat moderated, the impact of their descriptions would be less potentially harmful to the public perception and support of the real children and real families involved. This is a particularly important consideration when signs exist that children in schools today may graduate long before the public embraces the policies being advocated (if it ever does).

Educators, ranging from classroom practitioners to academic scholars or educational researchers, always write and speak from their own *perspective.* This perspective can create distance or closeness; it can build personal regard or foster interpersonal disdain. The human beings behind the data can be helped or hindered by the way information about them is disseminated. Of course, educators do have a professional perspective based on knowledge, experience, and expertise. However, their personal perspective, built on feelings, ambitions, and opinions, also influences their choice of data to select and describe. Successful reconstruction of educational language requires careful consideration of both professional and personal perspectives of all who write descriptively about children and families. Sensitivity to public perceptions being created, or even stereotypes being reinforced, is particularly important when *other people and other people's children are being described.*

A critical component of any educational perspective is a clear sense of professional responsibility. Giroux (1992) warns against habitual placement of blame for school failure outside the school. He suggests instead a habitual examination of the ways in which the school itself might be creating or reinforcing the conditions of failure. This does not mean that educators should be held responsible for social and economic problems beyond their control. It does mean that self-assessment is a critical key to educational reform.

Considering Other Perspectives. Nieto (1992) reminds educators that schooling is a dynamic process in which competing interests and values of student and community can be pitted against teachers and schools. Educators concerned with the language environment of their particular institutions should analyze the ways in which those competing interests and values are reflected in professional discussions. Do the educators in the institution acknowledge the existence of perspectives on problems other than their own, particularly in terms of sensitivity to the feelings of those students or families under discussion? If problems are discussed in ways that routinely locate them outside the institution, the language environment does not reflect an adequate level of professional responsibility.

Consider, for example, this hypothetical statement on the part of an educator: "The lack of parent involvement in this district is directly related to the learning problems and low test scores of the students." Whose perspective immediately emerges as dominant? It is the perspective of the educator alone that identifies and locates the problem. The perspective of the parents, who may be experiencing serious barriers to school involvement, is not reflected. Perhaps, for some parents or family members, the emotions attached to the memory of their own childhood difficulties in school impede their willingness to approach their children's teachers. But it is also possible that the district has not fully developed and articulated the concept of involvement for parents—is it advocacy, or political participation, or helping with homework, or occasionally asking the teacher about the child's progress, or volunteering? If asked to share their own perspective, the parents might say that they do not understand what the school expects of them and do not always feel welcome at the school. Perhaps a sign is posted on the front door of the school that says, *All parents and visitors must report immediately at the office; trespassers will be arrested and fined.* Or maybe a small group of parents joined together last year to question curriculum or discuss the homework policies of a certain teacher, and felt rebuffed by the school administration. Then again, the possibility exists that parents are being scapegoated for larger policy problems such as reduction of teaching staff, increased class size, or shortage of bilingual teachers. The lack of parent involvement, where it exists, may well be only one piece of a much larger educational dilemma.

Moving from the above example, how might the language of educators build a perspective that balances the tension of conflicting or competing demands? Educators need to create a base for problem solving by consistently balancing their own interpretation of cause and effect with the possible views of others involved. This balance can be achieved through routine use of educational expressions containing three components: (1) *sensitivity* to a variety of perspectives, (2) *accountability* for constructing solutions to problems, and (3) *inquiry* into causes and solutions of problems. To see how these three components might function together to improve the educational language environment, return to the original statement: "The lack of parent involvement in this district is directly related to the learning problems and low test scores of the students."

Rephrased to meet the three criteria of sensitivity, accountability, and inquiry, the same statement might change to this:

> We have to wonder if or how the continuing low scores and academic problems of the children are closely related to the fact that we have not yet reached our desired success in helping all our parents to become more involved in the education of their children.

This second statement discloses the same problems as the first (low test scores and the lack of parent involvement) but communicates sensitivity toward parents, accountability for the problem, and a sense of inquiry about the cause. If overheard by a parent, this statement would leave the door open for future dialogue and continued efforts toward mutual goals.

Now consider another example of a statement that poses a problem of language and perspective. Imagine an educator in a highly impoverished area saying this:

> Most of our children live in public housing projects, and are exposed to violence and an incredible host of social ills. This is undoubtedly related to their inability to reach national norms in reading and math.

Once again, it is the perspective of the educator alone that identifies and locates the problem. While there is a statistical connection between child poverty and low standardized test scores (Natriello, McDill, & Pallas, 1990), some of the causes of that connection undoubtedly exist within the school.

In this case, what might be the perspective of the children whose achievement difficulties are being blamed on housing and economic problems beyond their control? Perhaps they might say that they sense differences in the attitudes and expectations of their teachers—"As soon as they find out we come from the projects, they don't think we can be smart in school." Different children within those housing projects undoubtedly have different experiences. They could each share a perspective on how living in the projects affects their achievement: "I can't concentrate on my homework because of the shooting I hear at night," contrasted with, "My grandma helps me finish all my homework every single day." Now, imagine taking those very children on a field trip to a nearby suburban school with computers, a swimming pool, new books, and a beautiful playground. Small voices might well be saying, "Wow! I sure would do better if I had all these things in my school."

With sensitivity, accountability, and inquiry in mind, the original statement could be rephrased in this way:

> If life in those housing projects is as difficult as we think it is for many of our children, we need to learn more about how to reduce their

stress and provide the positive experiences that can enhance their test scores. It is so unfortunate that we do not have access to all the resources that would help them reach national math and reading norms.

Once again, the same information is provided as in the original statement. The perspective, however, is sensitive, accountable, and interested in solutions. Without this balance, educational language can be inflexible and unfeeling. It is crucial (although admittedly uncomfortable) for educators to face the fact that negative statements about students, families, and communities can weaken their sense of professional accountability, affect the thoughts and feelings of their students, and raise public questions about their own effectiveness and level of professional caring. The fundamental ethic that no child be harmed in the process of education dictates the importance of continual monitoring of educational talk.

Constructing Transformational Language

Language can serve as a barrier, but it also can serve as a powerful pathway to transformation of teachers, students, researchers, scholars, and all who serve in the field of education. Language is *transformational* when it opens possibility, provides enlightenment and understanding, and leads to the construction or reconstruction of agency and hope for all people (Grant & Tate, 1995). Educators who construct transformational language are always cognizant of the need for focus on intended outcomes that serve the good of teachers, students, and schools. They also respect the great power of language itself, which Postman and Weingartner (1969) describe as possibly the least visible but most profound environment for human interaction. The power of language exists in its *meaning*, so educators must be vigilant in reflecting on the true meaning of what they say. What is *meant* when children in an impoverished urban or rural public school are described as "that kind of kid," or when children experiencing disabilities are referred to as "our most limited population"? Such expressions set children apart and cut them off from the positive effects of being valued within the school. It is thus hard to deny the derogatory and potentially harmful meaning of such statements. I believe that the task before all educators is to employ words and meanings that denote that those who are described are *just like us in essential ways and just as valued as our own children and families.* The accomplishment of this task often requires educators to discuss the existing needs of students without designations that tend to stratify or set apart.

"Language," says Cuffaro (1995) is "the means by which we affect each other and ourselves in contemporaneous dialogues . . . the *how* of our connectedness, the way in which we come to possess things in common" (p. 25). A warm and humane language environment denotes close and valued relationships, even in large public institutions. In the greatest sense, transformational educational language supports the continued existence of democratic community—a community that protects the right of every member to acceptance, full inclusion, and access to the most valued outcomes of education.

ACTIVITIES TO ENHANCE UNDERSTANDING

1. *Language journal.* Observe the language environment of an educational institution for a designated period of time. Note specific statements made, and analyze them for meaning and repercussions for students.
2. *Language self-reflection.* Pay close attention to your own use of language about children and students in an educational environment. What biases or stereotypes come to your attention? Do you make habitual use of labels or educational designations? How do you respond to institutional stratification in your own language? What might you add to or change in the way you speak?
3. *Descriptive analysis.* Select a book or article that describes children who currently are experiencing some of the problems discussed in this chapter (e.g., poverty or abuse). What meanings are communicated, and what ramifications might result? Rephrase deficit-based descriptions to provide the same information while also expressing sensitivity, accountability, and inquiry.

2

Educational Language and Democracy: Social Responsibility, Morality, and Inquiry

Language is a powerful social phenomenon and thus a central vehicle for social responsibility. Chapter 1 proposed the conceptualization of educational language as an overt professional behavior that has a direct influence on all educational outcomes. It also suggested that educational language be constructed on two basic principles:

1. The ethical responsibility of educators to seek positive avenues for optimal development for all students; and
2. The democratic responsibility of educators to build commitments to equality and liberty into their professional practice.

Those two principles can help every American educator to formulate a personal response to an important question: Why should we care if children do not receive equal treatment and equal opportunities for excellent education in schools? The caring professional response inevitably will demonstrate strong connection to democratic ideals dictating that all relationships, including educational relationships, be characterized by a sense of fairness and equal opportunity. In order to explore the relationship of educational language to democratic ideals, this chapter will focus first on language as the basis of all social relationships, and then on the relationship of educational language to social responsibility, morality, and the construction of a just democratic society.

LANGUAGE CONSTRUCTS SOCIAL RELATIONSHIPS

Language is a social behavior. It cannot exist as an isolated phenomenon; rather it is *dynamic* in its constant interchange with all aspects of human life. Language has an internal characteristic of social meaning, which is why and how it builds social connections (Bourdieu, 1991). The power of language, however, does not end with meaningful construction of social connections. Language contains *intentionality* through its power to create desired outcomes and to influence relationships through shared social meanings (Putnam, 1994). All who speak, therefore, are not simply describing or responding to social events and relationships—they inevitably are *influencing* them as well. This is why educators must exercise vigilant reflection on the intentions and social outcomes of the words they use.

Imagine, for example, that two professors in different sections of the same course are each talking to their students about an upcoming assignment. Consider the subtle differences in their statements:

> Every one of you is competing for a grade, so keep in mind that only 15% of you can get an A. I suggest that you begin quickly to work on this assignment because only the fast starters will be able to find all the library resources they need.

> I understand that each of you may be feeling competitive with the others about grades, particularly because university policy dictates that only 15% of you can receive an A in this course. You will find it helpful to start to work on the assignment quickly. Also, try to obtain library resources early so you are certain of their availability.

Each statement is essentially communicating the same information: University grade policy creates a competitive environment; it is a good idea to begin work on the assignment quickly; and early gathering of library resources will ensure greater success. But there are differences in the *intentionality* as well as the *social dynamics* of the two statements. Statement one appears to utilize and build on inherent competition as a motivational strategy; statement two appears to recognize anxieties connected to inherent competition and to address them through suggestions for successful completion of the assignment. Although these statements are simple, they inevitably reflect differences in teaching philosophy. These professors were not *just talking* about the assignment—their words undoubtedly influenced the thoughts and feelings of their students about the assignments themselves and about one another in different ways. The most important concept for educators in thinking about language and social intentionality is that *words create contexts and influence all social situations.*

LANGUAGE, ORGANIZATION, AND CLASSIFICATION

Life-long human development calls for continual organization of information from the environment into new or preexisting structures of thought and understanding. Language is a great humanizing force in that process of organization. It defines the distinctive social characteristics of human beings, who use language to organize and understand their social lives. The concept of *kinship*, for example, can come about only through conceptual organization and lingual classification (Bruner, 1966). Likewise, the creation of *community*, and the definition of individual and group roles within a community, depends on shared understandings built through language. Ultimately, the social organization of human concepts leads to the *classification* of all people in social systems.

It is critically important for educators to think carefully about the human tendency to organize thought and experience through categorization and classification. Once this organization has taken place, people have strong tendencies to perceive reality in terms of the conceptual systems they have created. These tendencies make it likely that people will observe only what can be readily classified with names they already know and will overlook or disregard everything else. As Johnson put it: "We see with our categories" (quoted in Postman & Weingartner, 1969, p. 127). Educators must be particularly aware of human tendencies regarding language and classification because categorization of students is so widely prevalent in the public schools of the United States.

Schools as Linguistic Communities

People who use the same symbols and signs form *linguistic communities* (Bourdieu, 1991). Once formed, linguistic communities function with modes and patterns of communication that signify shared meanings. These shared meanings, particularly the *names given to the role and value of individuals*, construct the social environment of community life. Educators have the dual role of organizing their own linguistic modes and patterns, while they also develop systems of classification of students. These classifications tend to *name* the potential, achievement, and perceived value of the students. Whether educators in any individual school construct their own classification system (perhaps designing teams of students according to ability in different subjects) or adopt existing systems (perhaps standard special education terminology such as learning disabled or socially and emotionally disturbed), the names assigned to students make a difference. The process of naming performs many functions in any institution: It affects all participants as it selects, discriminates, identifies, locates, arranges, and systematizes. Language thus becomes a living behavior with the power to organize all conceptual understandings within any institutional community (Dewey & Bentley, quoted in Postman & Weingartner, 1969).

To reflect further on the power of classification systems in the linguistic communities of schools, it might be helpful to think about a hypothetical scenario involving a student teacher and a university professor. The student teacher has completed a wide range of innovative university courses and begun his assignment in the fourth grade of a large public school. During his preplacement conference with his supervisor, the student expressed enthusiasm and eagerness to apply all he had learned in the classroom. However, when observed by the university professor a few weeks later, the student was teaching a dull and unimaginative lesson involving commercially prepared worksheets. After the observation, the student teacher and professor reflect on the lesson.

"Larry, can you tell me why you decided to teach your lesson in this manner?"

"Well, Dr. Blair, I know you are going to say I should have been more creative. But I had to teach on the kids' level."

"What is their level, Larry?"

"They are very slow. When I got here, I was told it was not a very smart group. You should see their test scores. More than half are well below the national norm."

"Could we talk about some of the individual children? Who was that lively girl up front who kept raising her hand?"

"Oh, Kenya. She loves school and participates in everything."

"She was very articulate when she spoke to you, Larry. Are you really certain she is slow?"

"Well, she is in the slow class. They do have a bright class, and if they thought she could be in there I guess they would put her in there."

"Larry, do you think you would be teaching differently in the bright class?"

"Oh, yeah! I would love to be able to do all the great things we learned on campus."

Larry clearly has been affected by the classification system within this school. Although his university supplied him with a great deal of relevant preparation, once in the school he adapted his own thinking to the system of naming and classification within the school. His own intentions, his social interaction with his students, and the outcomes of his teaching thus have been shaped by linguistic categories.

Human possibilities are shaped in many ways by tendencies to organize and classify through language. Educators must reflect carefully on the power of their linguistic categories to affect human lives. Their power must be accompanied by full acceptance of the moral challenge to use all educational language wisely and well.

Accepting Responsibility for the Power of Language

The democratic vision of educators should have a strong influence on the use of classification and naming within educational institutions. Any existing taxonomy of human potential can be helpful or harmful. Classification systems can be organized to identify strength and growth in all individuals, or they can identify ability in some and disability in others. They can challenge social tendencies to stereotype, or they can legitimate prejudice and discrimination. At their worst, systems of linguistic classification can become a form of symbolic domination of some people over others—even serving to intimidate those designated inferior or unworthy (Bourdieu, 1991). At their best, they can become moral and ethical vehicles for the protection of the rights of all human beings to full development of potential. If educators seek development of language that reflects the spirit and goals of democracy in human classifications, that language possibly could be the most visible bearer, transmitter, and protector of the existence of democracy within all schools.

EMBRACING DEMOCRACY THROUGH EDUCATIONAL LANGUAGE

Considering the tremendous challenges facing children and teachers in America today, any educator who chooses to willingly engage in this difficult climate will need a fully developed philosophy to survive potential setbacks and discouragement. I believe that the philosophy of democracy, with its bias of equity and liberty, can serve as a driving force for professional commitment to the service of American children. Through the guiding principles of democratic goals, hope for every child can be infused not only into the language environment but into the total learning climate of every school.

Democracy and Possibility

Education is the process of acquiring the skills, values, and knowledge necessary for any individual to function as a competent adult and citizen in society (Natriello et al., 1990). Citizens living in a democratic society must be prepared to embrace interest in the public good and challenge contexts that destroy human possibility. They need to understand that democracy is *dynamic*. Its continued existence in any generation depends on the intentions and motivations of people in that current society—people who fully comprehend their own role in the fluid survival of democratic community.

> Democracy is neither a possession nor a guaranteed achievement. It is forever in the making; it might be thought of as a possibility—moral and imaginative possibility. For surely it has to do with the way persons attend to one another, care for one another, and interact with one another. It has to do with choices and alternatives, with the capacity to look at things as though they could be otherwise. (Greene, 1985, p. 3)

Democratic beliefs, founded in a commitment to possibility, continually can strengthen the resolve of educators to speak and act as though positive change can be created for American children and schools.

Connecting Educational Language to Democratic Beliefs

Educators have the power to construct the form and focus of their own professional language. The language they construct should be supportive of the democratic goals of the society in which they live. This is particularly true because educators have the responsibility to prepare children for empowered engagement in society and government. Since the United States has embraced democracy as its form of government, and since the public schools are governed by constitutional principles, democratic beliefs should be fully integrated into educational language. When this is the case, the talk of educators would be characterized by concepts of freedom: freedom to seek knowledge, freedom to develop, freedom to choose and to change, and freedom to be fully included in what is most valued within the educational institution. *Possibility*, which freedom creates and protects, should be evident in all professional designations, definitions, and characterizations of students and schools.

If the rights and freedoms most closely associated with democracy are interwoven into educational language, the expectation of equity for students and schools should be evident. Educators have the responsibility to be on guard for any linguistic indications that injustice or discrimination (although still sadly evident in the larger society) is acceptable in school environments. Since negative classifications of students present the dangers of discrimination, a truly democratic *habit or disposition of mind* should incline all educators toward a consistent focus on potential and promise. Hope for even the most disadvantaged or disabled students thus would be visibly present in every school language environment.

It is important at this point in the discussion of democratic educational language to discriminate carefully between real and artificial or contrived expressions of intent toward students and schools. Language insistent on reflecting human possibility need not pretend that serious harm has not come to children or overlook real ways in which bias and discrimination serve as barriers to equal access to educational opportunity. Indeed, educators who strive to maintain a vision of the possible for students often may feel angry, disappointed, or frustrated—with students, their peers, families, social and educational institutions, and even with themselves. No matter how great the struggle, however, their language can express a persistent commitment to protect the rights of students and to create the best climate for their continued growth.

Institutional responses to the legislation and policy that have emerged since the civil rights movement have at times generated systematic statements within institutions. The stationary of an urban school district might have *We Are an Equal Rights and Equal Opportunity School District* or *We Do Not Discriminate on the Basis of Race or Gender* printed on every page. How can educators respond to discrepancies between routinized statements of commitment to democratic practices when forms of inequity or discrimination are still present in social or educational institutions? Many public school districts, for example, that have equity departments or officers in place continue to utilize student tracking systems that mirror the socioeconomic, racial, and cultural stratifications present in society. These same districts also may have patterns of unequal funding between schools in richer and poorer communities. Imagine this example:

> Mrs. Serrato is a high school teacher in a large metropolitan area. She teaches in the neighborhood in which she herself grew up, which is characterized by poverty and violence related to drugs. As an active school parent in the district, she knows that the two high schools in the wealthiest neighborhoods have smaller class size, more computers, better uniforms for sports teams, and better recreational facilities. People often refer to the students in her school as "kids like that" or "problem kids." Entering the school faculty room one day, she sees that the lead article in the monthly district newsletter is titled, *Equality and Excellence Goals of District Ten*. "Who really cares," she asks herself, "about the truth? Our kids don't get an equal chance, and the district wants to pretend it isn't so."

Educators are discouraged by the discrepancies between policies claiming commitment to democracy and practices that reinforce inequality. Discouragement can become skepticism and alienation.

The problem of truth and integrity in the pursuit of democracy is a serious one. Educators who sense discrepancies within their schools must still maintain a focus on the *possibilities* inherent in democracy. Democracy is always in the making; a language of true intent to help recreate it can always lay the groundwork for social possibilities. Educators who are able to maintain a sense of possibility in their own professional language and practice will find themselves continually drawn to issues of equity because those issues are most reflective of the need for democratic responsibility.

The Relationship of Democracy to Educational Equity

It is not enough for educators to build principles of democracy into educational language. The integrity of democratic intent also requires educators to recognize existing inequalities and to strive to resolve them. In spite of over 40 years of articulated commitment to equal educational opportunity fostered by *Brown v. Board of Education* (1954), American public schools continue to be characterized by egregious inequalities (Kozol, 1991). The children whose social and economic needs are greatest are the least likely to receive excellent opportunities or adequate resources in public schools. It is ironic that programs that work well for all children are not provided for all children, and that services that counteract disadvantage are often least available to the disadvantaged (Bastian, Fruchter, Gittell, Greer, & Haskins, 1985).

The continuing struggle for school equity belies a basic sense of fairness in the distribution of goods and services within our social order (Edmonds, 1979). Rist (1970), in his enduring study of the relationship between teacher expectation and social class, notes that the public school system not only mirrors the configurations of the larger society, but also contributes to maintaining them. "Thus, the system of public education in reality perpetuates what it is ideologically committed to eradicate . . . class barriers which result in inequality of the social and economic life of the citizenry" (p. 449). It is easy to understand why the language of educators can fall prey to discouragement. But, rather than give in to that discouragement, educators can use their language to resist inequality and maintain a focus on hope and commitment to reform.

Equity and Activism. Democracy by its nature creates constant opportunities for engagement in the construction of a just society. Therefore, the language of educators can be an active response to the existence of inequity or injustice in schools or society. John Dewey's belief that "it is the business of everyone interested in education to insist upon the school as the primary and most effective interest of social progress and reform" (Archambault, 1964, p. 24), persists as a key to the construction of a democratic educational language. Dewey suggested that the school should be an ethical community—"a community which *wants* to know what is right and good" (p. 175) and organizes itself according to democratic standards and ideals. He also urged the school community to take a well-articulated public position on issues of reform.

Chapter 1 suggested that the presence of *inquiry* in the language of educators can support positive approaches to problems. When the language environment of a school is permeated with active inquiry, democratic questions about justice and fairness can evolve naturally. Educators thus might deal more readily with difficult questions: Why do some students have more school resources than others? How do we build and assess the presence of justice in our school? What questions do our students have about fairness and equal opportunity? These questions and many others create a *spirit* of democracy that can strengthen the level of engagement of educators and students in the social struggle toward equal opportunity. Students who get the sense of democratic commitments from the way the educators around them talk will be better prepared themselves to engage in the complex levels of thought and judgment required in a democratic society.

Democracy, Equity, and Risk. Democratic pursuits are not always comfortable. "The pursuit of equality has always been a difficult task; always misrepresented in various ways by those with a vested interest in maintaining the status quo" (Conway, 1992, p. 29). There is always a certain amount of risk involved in going against the grain to pose challenging alternatives to present conditions. An educational language environment that fosters habitual inquiry is more hospitable to these risks and more rewarding for those who seek a better future for children. Imagine, for example, the response to teacher inquiry in two different schools:

> Ms. Debnar, a new teacher in the Maple Heights Middle School, is attending the second yearly faculty meeting. The principal asks the faculty for assistance in setting the goals for the school year. Ms. Debnar states her concern about the number of children in her class who appear to lack appropriate clothing. She proposes several ideas: Teachers and parents could work together to have some kind of used clothing exchange in the school, and the guidance counselor could have a meeting with parents to be sure they were aware of available resources in the community. "Also," she says, "I think most of the children who are poor are in my class. Wouldn't it be a good idea for them to mix with all the children? I would like to suggest heterogeneous groups in a few subjects."

SCHOOL ONE

There is a silence after her comments, followed by a statement from the principal that she will talk with Ms. Debnar later about her ideas. In the ensuing conference, the principal supports Ms. Debnar for her compassion but reminds her that a school cannot provide social services. The principal further states that the children would be sad if exposed to the greater wealth of children in the higher groups and suggests that Ms. Debnar focus on her classroom instruction.

SCHOOL TWO

The principal asks for ideas and suggestions. Another teacher reminds the group about her visit to Appalachia several years earlier, and describes the used clothing exchange that she observed there. The principal says she has been concerned about the clothing problem for some time and suggests ways of getting used clothing donated without posing embarrassment to the parents. The Title I teacher says some parents in her group might be willing to take responsibility for such a project. The faculty acknowledges that most of the children in the low group are on public assistance, but do not agree on ways to combine classes. A committee is formed to discuss a possible heterogeneous activity and also to anticipate ways to help children develop a caring awareness of socioeconomic differences in the school.

The above examples contrast school environments where social activism is discouraged or encouraged, as well as environments where deeper issues like the socioeconomic dimensions of school tracking are silenced or discussed. Teachers in schools that silence and discourage activism may feel unable to take the risks necessary to raise critical issues. This is most unfortunate, because educators have access to broad knowledge about childhood disadvantage— knowledge of suffering and neglect of basic needs such as a home, food, or medical services for many students, as well as knowledge of institutional disadvantages created by forms of tracking. This knowledge should lead to professional discussion of social responsibility to alleviate suffering and inequity. "It is not good enough to favor justice in high literary flourish and to feel compassion for the victims of the very system that sustains our privileged position" (Kozol, 1990, p. 33).

Educators do enjoy a position of privilege when compared with many schoolchildren and families in America. While at times they may be exhausted by the daily demands they face and discouraged by the vast needs of their students, they do wield the power and possibility of schooling. If educators actively promote internal and external dialogue of responsibility to the social needs of children, the rewards of personal activism may be greater than the ultimate ramification of professional silence. Perhaps, in seeking ways to create a more just democracy for the students in their institutions, educators can find a renewed and invigorated moral voice of their own.

LANGUAGE AND MORAL MEANING

Democracy has the power to continually drive the moral dilemmas of a society to the surface. Educators in democratic institutions often encounter moral dilemmas that are closely related to the failure of the greater society to meet the needs of children and families. They also encounter moral dilemmas that are caused by discrepancies between the ideals of democracy and the realities of discriminatory or inequitable institutional practices. The professional preparation of many teachers, for example, stressed the importance of being fair to children and of valuing them on an equal basis regardless of background or ability. Once they began to work within educational institutions, however, many became aware of stratification of students accompanied by a significant difference in the provision of school resources. These and other discrepancies between the ideal and the real create the need for moral responses on the part of all educators. Teaching is a moral undertaking; the morality of teaching can be judged by "how we make ethical choices in situations that provoke deliberation and that culminate in a value judgment" (Cuffaro, 1995, p. 53).

Barriers to Moral Practice

Every educator today probably could point to some institutional barriers or restrictions that limit moral choice. There are often times when the requirements of professional positions seem to interfere directly with the best interests of students. University professors may be required to teach courses that seem outdated, to utilize problematic field placements for students, or to meet publication or research pressures that limit student–professor interaction. Classroom teachers may be pressured to produce high standardized test scores at the price of developmentally appropriate practice, to teach without adequate resources, or to teach students with special needs without supportive services. Public school administrators may be required to respond to budget restrictions by cutting important services for children, to spend an inordinate amount of time on paperwork, or to limit public comments about school problems to those permitted by the public information office of the district.

When challenges to moral practice exist, the educator is required to engage in an *internal moral discourse*. What do I personally think is *right*? How might I take an institutional or public stance on what I think is right? How can I engage in responsible dialogue with others? How can I responsibly communicate my ideas about moral practice to my administrators and colleagues? What are my choices, and how do I engage in them? Should I take a risk and make myself less comfortable in my institution in order to advocate for a change?

An internal moral discourse strengthens the sense of professional accountability crucial to external dialogue with others. Habitual reflection on the moral dimension of professional practice leads naturally to responsible participation in democratic institutions. A professor, for example, may decide to express concern about inadequate field placements at the next faculty meeting. A teacher might suggest the formation of a parent–school committee to discuss the need for increased resources. An administrator might suggest that a professional organization survey all the schools to find out how the budget cuts are affecting important services for children.

Active position taking is the antidote to a potentially disastrous professional slide into disenfranchisement and inertia. The educator must develop a strong sense of the moral professional role in a less-than-perfect institution. Without it, burnout and excuse making can destroy a democratic climate of *possibility*. The many children in our nation who have no choice but to function in a world that does not meet their basic needs deserve to be schooled in a climate of hope. Moral educators who do not excuse themselves from the struggle of those children, become democratic role models whose language environment can strengthen children. All problems cannot be solved. The morality of professionals exists not in the absence of problems but in the presence of positive intention and caring persistence. The vision and courage of educators, reflected in democratic school language environments, have the power to keep a sense of possibility alive for children of all abilities and circumstances.

The Power of Moral Service to Others

Educators committed to an ethic of caring about their students often may feel disempowered by the barriers they face. Difficult students, low budgets, troubled families, disgruntled colleagues, and other dilemmas can cause educators to question the efficacy and purpose of their own efforts. It can be helpful, therefore, to distinguish between power *for its own sake* and power *in the service to others* (Noblit, 1993). Power for its own sake seeks rapid results in the clear domination of problems. Such power can be fueled by ambition, the intention of making a strong impression on others, or the desire for control of a wide domain. Power in the service to others is less aggressive, more humble, and quietly persistent in the face of setback.

To care about others, to publicly disclose that care, and to act as though one cares have deeply enduring (not necessarily immediate or measurable) effects on those cared about. Service to others has many unknowns and thus is affected by countless circumstances beyond the control of those who desire to help. Success rests much more strongly, then, in the power of moral intention than in more elusive short-term results. This power must be well established in a language environment that supports and protects caring for others as a moral and ethical goal.

Consider for a moment the case of a hypothetical student named Johann, who has recently transferred into the large first grade of a suburban school. Johann has been placed in foster care because of a neglectful home environment and is being treated for clinical childhood depression. The length of time he will spend in the school is unknown; the goal at this time is to return him to his home after his parent completes outpatient addiction services. Johann, who had attended a school in a poor community, seems far behind most of his current classmates in academics and social development. The teachers on the first-grade team in the school, however, have discussed Johann and made strategic promises to one another. Since they each will have Johann for at least one subject, they are each committed to building a profile of his strengths. They each plan one personal and encouraging interaction daily ("Johann, let me just take a moment here to show you how much better your handwriting is than it was 2 weeks ago!"). Also, whenever the time does come for Johann to leave the school, they have decided to write a report on his strengths and areas of growth to send to his social worker and his new teacher in whatever school he attends. These teachers are dedicated to making sure that Johann's stay in their school makes a memorable difference in his life.

The intentions of these teachers have moral meaning because they seek to influence critical outcomes through their own sense of caring (Hansen, 1993). Their decision to care transcends the terribly discouraging circumstances of Johann's life—particularly the knowledge that he soon may return to a difficult life at home and a different school. Their caring also reinforces the humanity of the school environment and influences their relationships with their students as well as with one another. In great or small ways, Johann and many other students will sense their empathetic behavior and model it in future interactions. Even seemingly mundane or simple instrumental acts that are related to larger purposes take on a moral meaning, particularly when they are undertaken to have a formative effect on another human being (Hansen, 1993). Teachers are transformative (Giroux, 1988b) because the changes they seek in others are personal, developmental, and long lasting. Change that is centered in moral power and caring directs transformation to the greatest possible good.

The current social and economic challenges to the well-being of children make it critical for teachers to develop an intellectual willingness to acknowledge the nature of their struggles (Giroux, 1988a). The oppression experienced by students should be understood in social and historical context to avoid the danger that those who are oppressed will be blamed for problems well beyond their control. Zeichner (1992) urges educators to examine the social, economic, and political inequalities that underlie many of the educational problems they encounter. This examination should lead to participation in broader struggles to build a more caring and humane society. To try to see what is *wrong* (what currently interferes with student growth) and to take a position on what appears to be *right* (efforts that support optimal growth) can lead determined educators to the pressing task of building a democratic and humane language of inquiry and possibility in schools.

ENVISIONING AN EDUCATIONAL LANGUAGE OF POSSIBILITY

Democracy and morality are the underpinnings of an educational language of possibility. The vibrant activity of educational talk, deeply based in the ethics and caring of individuals, is laden with the greater contexts of experience, belief, and intention. But how can the day-to-day life of busy educators reflect an appropriate awareness of what is said? The answer lies in great part in the concept that *educators teach who they are.* It is thus far more in the act of becoming than the condition of knowing that educators transform themselves and others. Central to process of becoming is awareness of the presence of *generalization* and *inquiry* in the daily talk of educators. Generalization, an extension of the tendency to categorize people and experiences, can interfere with the transformative process. Inquiry, on the other hand, creates a climate of constant reflection on assumptions and beliefs. Part of that reflection must be a habit of caution against allowing bias or stereotyping to slip into habits of speech. The greater the reflectiveness, and the stronger the commitment to social justice, the greater the likelihood of powerful democratic reconstruction of the language of educators.

Transformation and Generalization

The tendency of human beings to classify and categorize information was discussed earlier in this chapter. At this point in the discussion of educational language, it may be useful to examine the problems of generalization. The tendency to generalize about students in school, which is related to issues of classification, may be the strongest threat to positive construction of an educational language environment. Transformation depends on an open view of possibility, which overgeneralization about students, families, and communities can undermine.

Most schools would be very chaotic places if educators did not organize the daily flow of activities. There is a familiar routine in many large public schools throughout the country: Buses pull up at designated doors, bells ring, lunch begins at a specified hour, stairwells have signs directing students to go up or down, and children traveling to the bathrooms might carry large wooden keys with classroom numbers on them. These routines, and many others like them, carry generalized expectations of behavior. If the school is to function on an effective level, everyone in it must know the policies and follow the rules. The needs of individuals are always subsumed into the larger context of the general order that must be maintained.

It is easy to see how generalizations routinely emerge in the life of institutions. Organizational environments that create the need for a focus on movement and maintenance of groups can foster a language filled with assumptions. In schools, these assumptions can be applied to different groups: grade levels, ability groups, and individual classrooms. Some generalizations may appear to be harmless ("The third grade seems so lively this year"), while others are troubling ("This is the worst third grade we've had in years"). All generalizations have the power to subsume the individual into the group and thus to attach inappropriate characteristics to some or all within the group. For example, the "worst third grade in years" may have three out of 36 children who are posing unusually difficult behavior challenges to the faculty. Two of these three children may be demonstrating daily improvement, and the third may be on a waiting list for limited psychological resources within the school district. Although the rest of the children are functioning well, the added challenges posed by a few has crept into generalized characterization of the entire grade.

On a more dangerous level of generalization, groups can be characterized as permanently deficient or devalued. Perhaps some of the following hypothetical statements appear familiar:

> If you think these kids are tough, you could never handle the kids in the north side schools.

> If you want to teach inner-city children, you must be prepared for difficult behavior problems.

> Our special education students are included in many school activities but they tend not to interact well with normal children.

> These children in foster care don't have the parental support necessary to maintain their grades in school.

In the statements above, generalization appears to have crossed the line to *bias*. Derman-Sparks (1989) defines bias as "any attitude, belief, or feeling that results in, and helps to justify, unfair treatment of an individual because of his or her identity" (p. 3). It is easy to see how bias in the above statements is potentially harmful to the students. Excellent teachers might be reluctant to pursue "north side" or urban teaching positions, children who have special education designations might be further excluded from school activities, or the school may fail to engage foster parents or other adults who are very interested in helping those children in school who live apart from their parents.

How might educators differentiate between true informational generalizations ("Our students all come from the south side, which is a lower-income area") and inappropriate, biased generalizations ("Parents on the south side have no interest in helping their children get to college")? First of all, they must fully acknowledge the continued presence of bias, prejudice, and discrimination in American society. Then they must reflect carefully on the distinct possibility that the bias that permeates society has affected their own perceptions of people and problems. (Yes, it is possible for all the students in the school to live in an area characterized as low-income. No, it is not possible that all parents in that area have the same level of interest in helping their children attend college. Why would that assumption exist, and *what are the harmful repercussions of such an assumption?*)

Postman (1979) makes two important observations: (1) It is always necessary to provide a balance to the information biases of a culture, and (2) it is the main business of education to know what the biases are and to know what to balance them with. In the previously mentioned case of bias about south side parents and the interest in college, the bias may be that *low-income parents didn't go to college themselves so they are less likely to care if their children go.* How can an educator balance such a bias? A good approach would be critical inquiry into the real circumstances of the parents under scrutiny. Have they been asked about their desires and interests concerning college for their children? Some may be saving resources on a regular basis, and others may indeed have gone to college (or very much wanted to) themselves. Some may be unaware of the opportunity provided by state and college financial aid, and others may not realize that their children are achieving on an academic level high enough to aspire to college attendance. Inquiry might reveal that the number of children from the south side who attend college has been steadily rising, thanks to the efforts of local community organizations.

While there is no easy way to be assured that bias has been eliminated from generalizations used in educational institutions, those educators who approach any tendency to generalize with caution can become more astute in their use of language. There may be some discomfort in moving away from the familiar; daily life is more uncertain when questions replace assumptions. However, when directives or absolutes are modified, educators accept the responsibility for choice and freedom and view themselves as capable of creating meaning in schools (Cuffaro, 1995). Statements of certainty ("The children in the emotionally disturbed class have little tolerance for stress") can be replaced with statements of inquiry ("I wonder why they become so stressed"; "I wonder how we might alleviate that stress"). It is questions such as these that lead the way to democratic talk in educational institutions.

Transformation and Inquiry

Transformative education consistently evolves toward reconstruction of experience (Miller, 1990). While the habitual talk and meanings of institutions may be resistant to change, they can still be enriched and enlarged through experience. Educators are, after all, continually challenged by their experiences to reorient themselves, resolve doubts, solve problems, and regain equilibrium. This process supports reflective thought, which progresses from belief to doubt to reflection to decision (Greene, 1973).

Educators open to reorientation of their own thinking about schools and students must seek dialogue with others. While many feel that they do not have time during busy days in schools for substantial conversation, it is possible that they can find spaces in their days when dialogue might take place (Giroux, 1988b). Even in the unfortunate absence of formal opportunities for collaboration, educators who take advantage of spontaneous opportunities can work together to strengthen habits of inquiry. An internal institutional dialogue, particularly one that supports people in their own diversity, helps educators to establish a voice of their own and to speak for themselves (Greene, 1985). The concept of dialogue presupposes the presence of inquiry. Whatever the challenge under discussion, and wherever the sources of problems, questions dominate the conversation. Inquiry can arise in many contexts such as class-rooms, hallways, teachers' rooms, faculty meetings, committee meetings, and all other formal or spontaneous opportunities for interchange.

To further reflect on the role of inquiry in educational dialogue, imagine that you are the parent of a child who recently has been diagnosed with a learning disability. While you recognize your child's needs for extra support, you also want to be absolutely sure that her teachers are aware of her strengths and abilities. During a conference regarding her individualized instruction plan, you probably would ask many questions: "Are you aware of the fact that she knows how to play the piano?" "If she is able to read some books, why is she having so much difficulty with reading in school?" "Do you think a loss of confidence has created some of these problems?" "Could her knowledge of music be used to help her develop better math concepts?"

In the dialogue created by your questions, you and the professionals at the meeting could seek answers to help shape important decisions about your child. You naturally would seek every assurance that the educators are respectful of you and your child and hopeful for all the possibilities in her future. You would not want the professionals to generalize about your child just because of her current diagnosis. As a parent, you would want to share your own understanding of the discrepancies between her strengths and weaknesses, and to build on her strengths to continue to develop her potential. Isn't it possible that she could outgrow her disability? Or might she become so strong in other areas that the disability would not have significant impact on her adult life? Through your questions you would be an inquiring individual who sought the best possible outcomes for your child.

It is the same level of inquiry that all educators hopefully could model in schools that support a democratic language environment. Cautious of assumption and generalization, caring educators should look for all openings to greater understanding and better solutions to the problems of children. An educational language focused on inquiry and strengthened by a moral commitment to implementation of democratic principles has the power to change the structure of schools. Within such a change, the hope and agency of all individuals could be validated.

ACTIVITIES TO ENHANCE UNDERSTANDING

Interviews of educators and students can provide meaningful insight into theoretical concepts. Plan to interview one or more educators and one or more children to explore diverse responses to some of the concepts developed in this chapter. Suggested concepts are the role of educational talk in schools, equity in schools, stratification and classification in schools, and democratic school practice.

1. *Interviews of educators.* Identify educators to interview informally. Design questions in the following two areas:
   - *Language, professional behavior, and equity.* Identify questions that could help educators explore their beliefs about the way their use of educational language influences their own behavior, particularly in terms of school equity. Sample questions might be: How do you usually describe children who are poor? What words are used in your school to talk about children who are behind national norms in math and reading? Can you give a list of terms or labels that tend to be applied to children in your school? Do you think that the way people talk about students actually influences student outcomes?
   - *Perceptions of democratic commitments.* Design a series of questions to ask educators about the relationship of democratic commitments to educational practice. Sample questions might be: How should democratic beliefs influence daily practice in schools? What is the responsibility of the school to children who are disadvantaged, disabled, or delayed in any way? Is the school responsible for challenging or resisting the ways children are stratified in society? Is tracking or grouping in the school fair to all children?

Analyze their responses to identify some key issues or discrepancies that emerge.

2. *Interviews of students.* Select some school or university students who are available for informal interviews. Design questions to learn about how they perceive systems of educational stratification.

   - For *younger children*, sample questions might be: Are there different groups of children in your school? How would you describe the children in these different groups? How would you describe your group? Do all the children in your school get to do the same things? Does everyone get the same chance to be smart and get good grades?

   - For *older students* (ideally in teacher education programs), sample questions might be: Do you believe that students should get equal opportunities in school? If so, how should the schools be organized to meet the needs of children with different backgrounds and different ability levels? What do you remember about school tracking and grouping from your own education? Were your schools fair to all students?

   Analyze the results of your interviews for issues, problems, or discrepancies.

3

Language and Practice in Educational Institutions: Seeking Democratic Recognition of Student Potential

This book is constructed to build the concept that educational language is a vehicle for social responsibility when it is founded on principles of democracy, morality, and inquiry. The present chapter will turn to a more specific examination of the interplay between educational language and democratic practice within public schools. The democratic goals of public schools were reinforced when the 1954 *Brown* decision established public education as possibly the most important function of state and local government. The Supreme Court delivered that powerful opinion based on the key assumption that no child could reasonably be expected to succeed in life without the opportunity of an education. Education, according to *Brown*, must be made available on equal terms to all children (*Brown v. Board of Education*, 1954). Moving from *Brown* to our current educational climate, I argue that a critical function of educational language in democratic public school settings is to continue to protect and uphold the right of children to the equitable opportunities that will give them equal access to success in adult life.

THE LANGUAGE OF PUBLIC SCHOOLING

The future of the American democracy depends on the thorough preparation of schoolchildren for responsible participation in civic activity. A critical role of the language environment in public schools, therefore, is the creation of a context in which children can develop their identities as future citizens. The ways in which children are perceived and described by educators in schools ultimately become ways in which they perceive themselves. The hopes of students for the future depend to a great degree on the hopes their educators hold for them in the present. These critical hopes of educators are expressed not only in what educators say within the confines of school buildings but also in how they represent their students in the greater society. Public dialogue about children can either enhance or diminish their future reception in society and subsequent access to opportunity for success.

The Mission of Public Education

Language plays a key role whenever or wherever education is taking place. The impact of educational language is neither more nor less important and powerful in a public school, private school, child-care center, religious school, or any other educational program. However, the *mission* of public education, which is the support and protection of the democracy through regeneration of a prepared and informed populace, is unique. It is the public schools that serve the great majority of American children and thus shoulder the largest responsibility for the provision of equal educational opportunity to our diverse child population. Therefore, the ways in which language functions within public schools, the ways in which those schools are conceptualized and described in the halls of higher education and government, and the ways in which they are represented throughout society all bear great importance. It is not only the future of our current child population but the enduring vision of democracy itself that rests heavily on America's conceptualization of public education.

The current social and political climate of dissatisfaction with public schools has inspired widespread calls for restructuring and reform. Underneath the surface of these calls, however, a question exists of whether American citizens have retained their historical commitment to public education as a foundation and means of preservation of the democracy. An accrual of evidence indicates that an increasingly ambivalent American public is distancing itself from the public schools—in fact and in spirit. Mathews (1996) reminds us the of original and enduring mandate of public education:

> Because schools and other educational institutions served larger public interests, all citizens were obliged to support them. That was the corollary implied in the mandate. Because public schools were our agents for creating the kind of country we wanted to live in, they merited our allegiance. That was the logic of the contract with the public, the basis for a special relationship between the citizenry and the schools. (pp. 12–13)

In reflection on the above mandate, Mathews suggests that the continued bonds of broader social, economic, and political objectives tied to public schools have lost their power to inspire broad social commitment. Where do educators stand in relationship to this flagging response to the historical mandate of American public education? Are they also ambivalent, or do they embrace an ongoing responsibility to articulate commitment to democratic principles in public education?

With the above questions in mind, the prior discussion of ways in which *what educators say affects public opinion* re-emerges for serious consideration. The challenges faced by educators are unquestionably great. Educators must adjust to the enormous demands posed by our child population, retain a sense of efficacy in the midst of a loss of public interest and confidence, and yet publicly *reaffirm* the principles of democracy on which the traditions of public education have been built.

American educators, although understandably discouraged by indications of public disassociation from the needs of children and schools, can and should play a strong role in encouraging maintenance of the historical commitments to public education. Unfortunately, the voices of educators can be undermined in this difficult political climate by suspicion that they are motivated mainly by a self-interested desire to maintain their current sources of employment and income. While such suspicions are painful to educators who are earnest in their commitment to the democratic possibilities inherent in public education, they also serve as a reminder of the public importance of educational language. Educators need to constantly articulate their beliefs and commitments to the constituents of public education. The highly visible public discourse of educators should represent accountability to schools and children, while it also urges the public to focus on commitment to the welfare of all children in a democracy. Since there is an all-time high enrollment of 51.7 million students in public schools, it is clearly both prudent and moral that society help all those students to flourish (Good, 1996).

"But how," the skeptical taxpayer might ask, "can the kinds of children we keep hearing about and reading about in the public schools really flourish? Guns! Violence! Lack of motivation! Lack of family support! Why should we keep supporting schools that can't solve their problems and can't produce decent standardized test scores?" As pointed out in Chapter 1, such comments are, in part, an unfortunate result of the inundation of criticism of public schools as well as the deficit terminology about children that has permeated a great deal of discourse about the children in public schools. The sentiments underlying such comments sometimes reflect a lack of realization that it will take long-term and determined efforts on the part of all Americans to resolve some of the problems of children and families, which become apparent in the school setting. The active and positive discourse of educators, however, has the potential to help rekindle public enthusiasm to address these serious problems. What is most needed is a convincing argument that successful public education is more important now than ever before in history.

The Mandate of the Public Schools

The shifting tides of family life, the reality of serious troubles that many children face, the context of critical reflection on public education, and political manipulation of educational issues all create challenges for public education. The public must be guided in a rediscovery of the traditional mandate that expected public schools to

> Create and perpetuate a nation dedicated to particular principles, such as individual freedom and justice; Develop a citizenry capable of self-government; Ensure social order; Equalize opportunity for all, so that the new nation would not perpetuate Europe's class divisions, and Provide information and develop the skills essential to both individual economic enterprise and general prosperity. (Mathews, 1996, p. 12)

These goals continue to be relevant to the needs and interests of American citizens today. The fact that standardized test scores of some students have plummeted or that poverty in the lives of some students has soared provides a moral opportunity to examine the *reasons* why success and prosperity for some have declined. Widespread finger pointing about the causes of student failure only deters the public from honest examination of emergent democratic questions. In the absence of reflective thought, the quick fixes of accountability schemes, testing, and more stringent accreditation emerge. Simplistic and ultimately unproductive thinking about ways to monitor, scrutinize, and measure students and teachers can result only in a dizzying array of numerical scores—not in deep and rational approaches to important problems (Giroux, 1988a).

No one would rationally suggest that it would not be highly commendable if all American children achieved high scores on standardized tests. However, since so many children are falling short of national norms, a productive approach to national discourse about test scores is very important. The concern should be focused on the overall state of a nation in which children seemingly cannot thrive, and not on *blaming* children and teachers for the ramifications of complex national problems. What should educators and a concerned public look for in a national discussion of the current achievement problems of children? The first line of criticism, when such is expressed, should be aimed at the causes of childhood disadvantage. When issues such as *competition* and *standards* are substituted for basic concern about the conditions that challenge the development of children, public concern about the welfare of children is unduly averted.

Is it appropriate, after all, for current policy makers to demand *world-class schools* when social and economic conditions of American children make such a poor showing in cross-national comparisons (Taylor, 1996)? Is it appropriate for reformers to question the commitments and skills of teachers in schools that lack desks, books, paper, and basic utilities such as plumbing and heat? The central debate about schools should focus first and foremost on issues of social justice worthy of a democratic nation. Whatever educational reforms *unquestionably* are needed, the performance of all American children undoubtedly will improve when their society provides a kinder and healthier foundation for their ongoing development as valued human beings.

Focusing Democratic Dialogue About Children

Educators who understandably feel threatened by the tone of public complaint about schools and teachers might easily fall prey to resentment and inertia. They certainly could point to all the problems and shortcomings of children, families, and communities that interfere with school performance and test results. Their determined choice to rise to a disciplined and informed approach to the problems they face, however, can spark a responsible and democratic social debate.

An example of such a debate is the one posed by Natriello (1996), who challenges school critics to address the lack of resources and the inequities that affect educational outcomes for children. Natriello points out that about 14 million students attend the one-third of American schools that require extensive repair, and that 40% of America's schools lack the facilities to meet the requirements of large-group instruction or laboratory science even moderately well. He seeks to provoke a public response to problems of inequity that undoubtedly lead to some of the disappointing performances seen in some schoolchildren:

> The central problem of U.S. education at the end of the 21st century is not the lack of standards or the barriers to implementing technology.... The central problem of U.S. education is insufficient and unequal distribution of educational and economic opportunities, and in the development of this problem, both the corporate and the governmental sector have played major roles that the leaders of both sides seem to forget. (p. 7)

Natriello's focus provides a welcome relief from the barrage of complaints about children and teachers, and leads the reader to awareness of important issues. His words create an avenue for democratic dialogue about the responsibility of corporations and government for the creation of schools where optimal learning conditions exist.

The politics of American education emerge clearly in debates about the current status of public schools. These politics are "the substantive and procedural bases for deciding the distribution of educational resources, defining the uses to which schools are to be put and establishing the criteria by which schools are to be evaluated" (Edmonds, 1979, p. 16). Educators themselves must take a position on each of the many levels of political discourse. Some may speak to the issues on policy levels or in university classrooms, while others enact political positions in their daily interchange with children and colleagues in American public schools. The use of language on every level of the dialogue is of critical importance, whether it advocates for democratic principles of justice and equality in the distribution of resources or reflects belief in the resiliency and potential of the children who currently are denied adequate resources in school.

Of course, educators have a right to care about the status of public schools in part because their own work, income, and personal resources are closely tied to the successful continuation of public schools in America. They also have a right, however, to articulate to the public that they were drawn to their field by a sense of service and a willingness to spend their adult lives accepting responsibility for the growth and development of others. The fact that the work of educators is strongly centered in the concept of human service can support their articulation of a deep and enduring commitment to public education.

For example, consider the leadership of a hypothetical teacher named Esther, who is in her sixteenth year of public school teaching in a large urban area. Over the years some of her students have been arrested, and some have been killed or have died of drug overdoses. She has been unable, in spite of persistent efforts, to help all her students to achieve national norms in reading and mathematics. Furthermore, Esther cannot remember a year when she had enough books, desks, and supplies for all the students in her classroom. As union representative of her school, Esther is often in the position of making public statements about her school and students. She always begins by saying, "I am a human service professional, and I am deeply committed to the success and well-being of my students." An outspoken advocate for smaller class size, improvement in building upkeep, and increased resources for students (particularly guidance and psychological services), she sometimes encounters resistance. "The taxpayer is already supporting teacher salaries higher than the average income of this community. Why can't the teachers be the ones to help the students?" "Teachers keep asking for more and more money and resources but student achievement never goes up."

Esther carefully articulates her support for holding teachers and schools responsible for excellent efforts, while also encouraging public awareness and discussion of larger problems.

We teachers are committed to making every possible effort to ensure the success of our students, and we appreciate public input. We also want the public to know that good resources and supportive services for our students also build better schools and help us to boost achievement. Education needs the involvement of everyone in our community.

Esther thus is able to advocate strongly for students and to articulate her sense of professional accountability, while also urging the public to face its responsibilities in helping educators to create successful schools.

Why should all citizens care about the survival of public schools? They should care because every American institution and practice based on the premise that a system of common schools can accomplish a multitude of public objectives is at risk when our schools fail (Mathews, 1996). All citizens should be concerned, but educators can be the strongest voice advocating for the needs of students in public schools. This voice, first of all, can stand strongly for the rights of children to excellent and equitable educational opportunities. Second, it can continually remind the public that the children who receive humane treatment, adequate resources, and fair opportunities today are much more likely to be the responsible, productive citizens in the democracy of tomorrow.

> Public schools are the cornerstone of America's future. The public development of youth's knowledge, skills and appropriate affective and social dispositions has always been critical to the country's success. If it is possible, American youth will become even more important to this country's survival and welfare. By the year 2025, one out of five Americans will be 65 years or older. In less than 15 years, the first baby boomers will reach the age of 65. Clearly, the economic success of America will be in the hands of youth to an *unprecedented* extent. Investments in education should be applauded as a powerful strategy for continuing to maintain the American way of life. (Good, 1996, p. 6)

Educational issues are complex and difficult. However, educators have no choice but to confront them in comprehensive ways. Thinking back for a moment to the discussion in Chapter 2, it is important to reflect again on the need for ethical discourse that reflects the principles of democracy. Children can be surrounded by *opportunity*, so central to the palpable presence of democracy, only when their educators lead the public into a positive social and political vision of the continuing need for excellent public education.

LANGUAGE, TEACHING, AND LEARNING

Public schools in America have the potential to embody the great aspirations of our democracy, while they also provide daily opportunities for learning.

The current questions about the role of public education in America are paralleled by debates about what constitutes a valuable learning experience and what should be learned in school. Many different opinions exist on such concepts as back-to-basics, outcomes-based education, and developmentally appropriate practice, among others. Debates about the form and content of school curriculum have social, political, and educational ramifications. What remains certain in this multifaceted climate of school debate is that *teachers* themselves continue to be the most important key to what is done and what is learned in school.

> Teachers are among the most important influence on the life and development of many young children. They play a key role in creating the generations of the future. With the decline of the church, the break-up of traditional communities and the diminishing contact that many children have with parents who can "be there" for their children on a regular basis, the moral role and importance of today's teacher is probably greater than it has been in a long time. (Fullan & Hargreaves, 1996, p. 18)

Teachers as the Curriculum

Many think of learning in schools as centered in the curriculum, thus relegating teachers to the job of transmission of curriculum-based information. This common view overlooks critical ways in which teachers *become* the curriculum in terms of their attitudes, behaviors, and constant example to their students. Excellent teachers study and interpret the curriculum, bring it to life, model it, and embellish it with an eager desire for students to learn successfully. Teachers who lack critical skills and attitudes have the negative power to diminish the learning situation with low expectations, bias, boredom, lack of depth, and absence of real caring about student performance. The public debate over learning and curriculum must not overlook the fact that the characters and commitments of teachers have the greatest impact on what is learned in school. Children are fortunate when they attend school in the presence of adults who are passionate about their teaching and committed to optimal educational experiences for all children. There is no substitute for a teacher and role model who truly cares, who seeks success for the student, and whose own behavior reflects deep regard and respect for all others.

Talk About Teachers

Like all educational language, public dialogue about classroom teachers is always deserving of moral and democratic analysis. The current climate of general complaint about schools can lead to bias against teachers ("Education students have lower SAT scores; we need to attract better and brighter people to teaching") or to scapegoating of teachers ("The problem with the schools is that unions have protected the jobs of incompetent individuals"). While professional problems do exist and must be addressed, it is important to be ever mindful of the fact that classroom teachers are the most visible extension of the *entire profession*. Their strengths and shortcomings are best discussed in a context that unites classroom teachers with all others who are responsible for schools and education. If some teachers are indeed struggling, why is this the case? How effective was the quality of their undergraduate preparation? How committed were their colleges and universities to providing excellent resources to their faculties and academic departments? Were their college courses realistic in terms of the challenges they would encounter once in the field? Have their colleges and universities continued to support them and their professional interests? Have the experts who shape curriculum and research demonstrated true respect for them? Do political and administrative decisions in their districts and schools reflect concern for them as human beings? Is their excellence recognized and rewarded? These and many other questions should be examined by all who engage in dialogue about the performance and quality of classroom teachers.

Everyone in the profession of education should willingly share full responsibility for the influence of classroom teachers on children. If classroom teachers are failing to meet national goals and standards, for any reason, their failure should be shared by all who lead and influence them. These teachers are not just the daily representation of the total effectiveness of the profession—they (along with children) are the heart and soul of the very existence of the profession. Classroom teachers enact daily the shared vision of all who wish to change and improve education for children. The choices they make—about what to confront, what to question, and how to act—create the condition of education for their students (Cuffaro, 1995). It is thus tremendously important for any critics of teachers to see their role as one of supporting and strengthening teachers. They are the people who deliver the quality of the profession on a daily basis to the children of this nation.

Fostering Child Resiliency

While it is true that talk about teachers should be sensitive and inclusive, it is also true that the seriousness of the daily responsibilities of teachers must be fully recognized. Teachers can enhance or harm the lives of children every single day. It is thus important to turn the discussion now to the ways in which teachers themselves use language as the medium for exchange of learning and for relating to the children in their care. Bruner (1966) described teacher language ultimately as the "instrument that the learner uses himself in bringing order into the environment" (p. 6). Children thus conform to the identity constructed by classroom language and ultimately talk themselves like the kind of person they see themselves as being (Smith, 1990). This presents a highly compelling argument for morality and caring in the daily language of teachers; their students ultimately become an embodiment of what is said about them in schools.

As Sockett (1993) points out, it is *moral* words that describe with any proper depth what a profession is and does. For classroom teachers, words such as "*courage, honesty, kindness, carefulness, patience, compassion*" (p. 13), among others, capture the deeply personal moral mission of classroom teaching. Educators who use strong moral words to conceptualize themselves and their responsibilities bring powerful meaning and intent to their classrooms. Such words bring continual focus to the fact that classroom teaching is a critical human service profession. Sadly, national debates about standards and school reform can overlook the key role of caring human interaction in learning and teaching. The language of educators (and the enactment of that language in classroom actions and intentions) inevitably invokes deep emotional responses in students—responses ranging from alienation and despair to hope and human connectedness.

Spirited and caring words are so important in a social climate where so many children experience problems of a compelling and sometimes devastating nature. The real young children behind the oft-repeated statistics—those who are homeless, deeply depressed from multiple foster care placements, distracted by fear and violence, delayed by malnutrition or exposure to drugs in utero—all face an incredibly taxing emotional task. They somehow must come to see themselves as capable not only of basic survival but of eventually becoming adults whose lives are far better than current circumstances might dictate. And, lest only some children might be singled out, national statistics and events dictate recognition that all children are endangered by the possibility of addiction, violence, suicide, and other negative ramifications of social ills. *All* students today need their teachers to give strong and focused direction into a *possible* and hopeful future.

The unhappy truth is that many children may not have (or may not feel that they have) a logical reason to believe in themselves or their world. To compound such a sad state of affairs with school talk or practice that reinforces their hopelessness or deep sense of disenfranchisement raises fundamental moral and ethical questions. Teachers who actively confront the danger of reproduction of student despair must go far beyond simplistic considerations of student self-esteem. Talk and action within the institution must be designed to carry the hearts and minds of impressionable children into what might be available and might be possible. This necessarily would involve helping children to build, recognize, and value their own competencies. It also would require the strong vigilance of reflective educators determined to create a climate for *challenge and change* in the face of difficult circumstances. Teachers would need to argue that

> the what, when, and how of schooling should enable all children to break with their everyday experiences and . . . provide such a range of ways of seeing, knowing, thinking and being that it will be equally challenging to all students and teacher to imagine other possibilities, take risks with learning and transcend the boundaries of the immediacy of personal experience. (Heath & Mangiola, 1991, p. 17)

It is the imagining of possibility, so deeply connected to the principles of democracy, that can structure an institutional language of hope and respect.

Emotional Intelligence and Resiliency. Teachers should think carefully about the emotional effects of the language they use in schools. Language has an emotional effect not just on students but on staff, administrators, and other teachers. Particular attention in educational environments should be paid to ways in which language can strengthen the emotional intelligence of children. Goleman (1995) describes emotional intelligence as a different way of being smart in school. Children develop emotional intelligence by knowing and using their feelings to make competent decisions, manage distressing moods, and control impulses. They also develop it through intrinsic motivation, optimism, and skills in promoting positive human relations. It is easy to conceptualize links between emotional intelligence and *resiliency* in children. The repeated documentation of resiliency—the ability to bounce back and thrive despite exposure to severe risks—clearly indicates the self-righting nature of human development (Bernard, 1993). The emotional lessons that children learn in school quite literally shape their brain circuits for responses that can manage anger, be empathetic, and develop other important lifelong strengths (Goleman, 1995).

In today's complex society, all schoolchildren need their schools to provide more than academic basics. They need to know how to survive and overcome their daunting personal challenges, or how to manage their lives in a world where so many others are experiencing need or loss. All schoolchildren are going to live in an adult world that will be deeply affected by current social, economic, and political forces. An argument could be made that their emotional strength will be just as important as their academic accomplishments. This brings a special urgency to the need for ethical scrutiny of ways in which the educational language environment does or does not promote a spirit of resiliency in teachers and children. Even if statements, such as "the majority of these students will never complete high school" or "most of these children are crack babies who will have a lifetime of problems," are made out of the hearing reach of children, they damage the emotional and professional climate of the school. Resiliency cannot be fostered in schools when the adults within them have given up—or talk as though they have given up—on the children.

Talk About Student Classification. Chapter 2 of this book discusses the fundamental relationship of language to conceptual and experiential classification. Since student classification has retained a central role in many educational institutions, it continues to be important for teachers to examine the ways in which they discuss it. Many American children, as early as preschool or kindergarten, are classified and assigned to groups or tracks that contain other students of assumed similar ability. Some of this early classification is related to the need for special educational services, some is related to admission to private schools, and some is related to entry-level assessment in public schools. Assessment, classification, assignment to groups, and subsequent access to varied educational opportunities continue throughout the school careers of many students. While there has been intensive debate about tracking and grouping in educational research and literature, tracks and groups in many schools have remained unchanged. Thus, the ethics of talk about classification remains a central consideration of the school language environment. How does the discussion of student classification interfere with democratic possibilities for students—with their freedom to change and their equal access to what is most valued in the school environment? How do labeling, grouping, and tracking in any given school setting affect the emotional intelligence and ultimate resilience of children?

On the surface, it so often appears sensible to allow children to work with others on their current levels of achievement in order to enhance peer support and teacher efficacy. Years of research, however, have strongly indicated that grouping of students in many cases opens them to bias and subsequent alteration of access and encouragement. Tracking literature strongly suggests that low-track students receive a poorer quality of instruction, with lower expectations for performance, dull curricular materials and instructional techniques, and slow-paced instruction (Natriello et al, 1990). Oakes (1986) cites research indicating that White children are less likely than children of color to be placed in lower tracks, that children in high tracks have greater access to high-stakes knowledge, and that there is a discernible difference in the quality of classroom learning opportunities between higher and lower tracks. Such discrepant circumstances invite questions of discrimination because they are so likely to deepen the problems and reduce the resiliency of children already suffering marginalization or disadvantage in society.

The unbalanced opportunities created by grouping or tracking are unfortunately fertile ground not only for stereotyping and discrimination, but for unimaginative educational practices. Goodlad (1984) suggests that educators who continue to allow the unequal circumstances of tracking are giving up on the problem of variability in human learning. This represents a retreat from a challenge rather than a fair and intelligent strategy for approaching complex problems. Goodlad also refers to the notable differences in teacher expectations for low and high tracks as a capitulation to the admitted challenge of helping widely diverse groups of children to achieve educational outcomes reflecting their highest potential.

The important study of teacher expectation, which focuses on the inferences that teachers make about the future behavior or academic achievement of students based on what they know now about those students (Good & Brophy, 1987), is central to the problem of educational language in schools. Page (1991) asserts that conventional studies of teacher expectation often have overlooked the importance of the ways in which teachers actually *talk* about curriculum differentiation:

> Talk is action. What people say to each other in classrooms, schools and communities both echoes and structures their scholastic and sociocultural relations. Whether the talk is explicit or obscure; whether it is undertaken in lessons, faculty lounges, national reports, . . . people *use* words to talk into existence relations of difference and membership in scholastic and social orders. (p. 243)

Possibly the most convincing example of the problem of teacher talk about student classification was reported by Rist (1970) in his longitudinal study of student social class and teacher expectations. After establishing a strong connection between the socioeconomic status of children at the time of school entry and the initial teacher-designated ability groups, Rist established a clear connection between the original groups and the subsequent second-grade reading groups. He interviewed the second-grade teacher to explore her expectations for the children in the three reading groups: *Tigers* (top), *Cardinals* (middle), and *Clowns* (bottom). The following teacher responses unmistakably reflected the power of expectation based on grouping:

Concerning the Tigers:

Q: Mrs. Benson, how would you describe the Tigers in terms of their learning ability and academic performance?
R: Well, they are my fastest group. They are very smart. . . .
Q: Mrs. Benson, what value do you think the Tigers hold for an education?
R: They all feel an education is important and most of them have goals in life as to what they want to be. They mostly want to go to college. (p. 436)

The same questions were asked of Mrs. Benson concerning the Cardinals: . . .

Q: Mrs. Benson, what value do you think the Cardinals hold for an education?
R: Well, I don't think they have as much interest in education as do the Tigers, but you know it is hard to say. Most would like to come to school, but the parents keep them from coming. They either have to baby sit or their clothes are dirty. These are the excuses the parents often give. But I guess most of the Cardinals want to go on and finish and go on to college. A lot of them have ambitions when they grow up. It's mostly the parents' fault that they're not at school more often. (p. 437)

[Regarding the Clowns:]

Q: Mrs. Benson, how would you describe the Clowns in terms of their learning ability and academic performance?
R: Well, they are really slow. You know most of them are still doing first grade work. . . .
Q: Mrs. Benson, what value do you think the Clowns hold for an education?
R: I don't think very much. I don't think education means much to them at this stage. I know it doesn't mean anything to Randy or George. To most of the kids, I don't think it really matters at this stage. (p. 437)

It is poignant to reflect on the fact that the above comments are being made about children who are probably 7 years old in the second grade. Mrs. Benson is making a strong statement about herself as a professional whose preparation probably has not emphasized a language of inquiry, hope, and accountability. She does not wonder aloud about the differences in current interest and ability; nor does she indicate intention to rectify current differences. Rather, Mrs. Benson communicates an assumption of permanence, even to the point of predicting interest in college attendance in the young children she is teaching.

It is refreshing to imagine a differently oriented Mrs. Benson talking about equity and fairness—perhaps noting the socioeconomic differences among the three groups of children and searching for ways to make the school experience more equitable. The reality of what Mrs. Benson says about the Clowns, who have been demonstrated in the study to be the least advantaged children in the room, is of necessity disturbing. Her comments are far from "just talk." One must wonder not only about differences in the daily treatment of these children, but about the possibility that Mrs. Benson's beliefs lead to professional behaviors that virtually ensure that the children on the bottom will never have the chance to change that status. This is the *essence* of the problem of teacher expectation: What Mrs. Benson believes will have a direct impact on what her students ultimately achieve.

As I have pointed out before, educators pondering the implications of the above scenario need not conclude that it is necessary to deny either individual differences in children or harmful effects of poverty and other serious childhood challenges. The important point is that a *verbal habit of inquiry* can eliminate permanent and biased assumptions and keep doors open to future possibilities. A sense of accountability and a question of fairness should exist in any educational conversation about classifications, most particularly because student classifications are so consistently biased against children who reflect diversity or disadvantage. The desire to locate competency and use it to foster growth must consistently override a tendency to generalize about ability.

The negative effects of classification and grouping can be reduced when educators demonstrate the habit of *wondering aloud* about its rightness and actual helpfulness. From an ethical standpoint, it is important to wonder about the continued practice of using indicators of achievement and ability (IQ tests or standardized tests) that so consistently relegate diverse and less advantaged populations of children to the lower end of the classification system. In the absence of an intellectual challenge to these practices, one must wonder if some educators either desire to believe that some children are consistently inferior, or use classification systems to justify discriminatory actions. An understandable discomfort emerges with such questions, particularly if the children of educators themselves are among the groups that tend to benefit from high classifications and more resources and advantages within schools.

Wondering aloud about the rightness of classification and grouping also can help educators avoid harmful tendencies to make assumptions of *permanence* in the abilities of children who are actually in rapid stages of development. The child who may be experiencing fetal alcohol effect also may have remarkable musical abilities. The child who has been upset for the past few years about multiple foster family placements may have been placed recently with a loving family that plans to adopt him. The child whose desperate fear of failure has made it impossible for her to pass mathematics may just have successfully completed a Girl Scout workshop designed to support female mathematics abilities. Only those educators who have a determined habit of inquiry and an open mind to possibilities are likely to discover and capitalize on windows of opportunity when they emerge in the lives of children.

EXAMINING THE INSTITUTIONAL RATIONALE FOR CLASSIFICATION

Institutional power to name the present and future potential of human beings carries an awesome responsibility. Justification for uses of classification should be routinely re-examined, particularly when classification limits the opportunities of children. Tradition ("This is the way it has always been done") and intuition ("The school seems to function best when we do it this way") are never adequate rationalizations for policies that can interfere with the full development of some human beings. Even educational or psychological theory, often assumed to be scientific, may be outmoded or misused in the school setting. Bourdieu (1991) notes that theory can produce language that favors some aspects of reality while ignoring others. Institutional practices of classification and labeling based on theory and/or research should be implemented only after careful consideration of potential bias.

Research and Institutional Practice

Educators with a sense of inquiry can examine theory and research to determine whether they are open to many dimensions of human life and experience or if they have a more exclusive focus on experiences or characteristics of certain people. A study of children who are experiencing poverty, for example, can be constructed to examine delays, disadvantages, and disabilities related to economic hardships. Because poverty is detrimental to children, it is highly likely that the study will discover and communicate the problems of children who are poor. The process of research, and dissemination of the results of research, can reinforce deficit-based models of children experiencing economic disadvantage. But has the entire story been discovered and told?

No sensible person would propose that poverty has benefits for children, but many children who are poor do have tremendous strengths—perhaps resiliency following trauma, responsibility in caring for siblings or neighbors, willingness to make a great effort in school in spite of illness or exhaustion, religious faith, or a strong and hopeful certainty that they can overcome the problems in their lives. Just as important, many children who are poor could make rapid and meaningful gains if they had *access to appropriate support services.* If their strengths are unexplored, and their lack of access to supportive services unmentioned, then such important components of the total picture would not become part of the professional language generated by the research. Compare the following two statements:

> Thus, it can be concluded that the children who lived with single parents in low-income housing projects suffered the greatest cognitive effects as reflected in teacher reports, standardized testing, and school grades. Many appeared distracted or tired in school, and almost none of the children took part in after-school clubs or activities.

> Thus, while the children who lived with single parents in low-income housing projects were having difficulty in school, particularly in standardized and teacher-based assessments, many also reported a desire to work hard and improve. Over two-thirds of these children were highly

responsible in meeting significant home responsibilities, and many attended school daily in spite of exhaustion. The majority of the children did not have access to after-school child care or regular medical and dental services.

While the first statement might create an institutional justification for continued classification and grouping, the second would be more helpful to inquiring educators seeking to open more doors of opportunity for children who currently were hampered not only by poverty but by lack of resources and institutional assumptions of cognitive inferiority.

The Social Construction of Institutional Classification

All established and widely accepted knowledge signifies some kind of ordered meaning but also is open to *applied interpretation.* Objective understanding of educational theory and knowledge should be accompanied by an examination of the way in which such theory or knowledge is used in the process of education. Wittgenstein, quoted in Rhyle (1963), acknowledged this when he said, "Don't ask for the meaning, ask for *the use*" (p. 143). For example, research indicating that children who are poor enter school with delayed physical maturation and interrupted cognitive development might be used to justify *providing them with more resources and opportunities than those received by advantaged children.* The same research, however, can be overtly or covertly used as a rationale for the placement of children who are poor in lower-track classrooms where they get fewer resources and more limited opportunities (as is often the case in American schools). Bourdieu (1991) reminds us that acts of institutions embody a special form of communication. These acts signify to someone what his or her identity is and impose it on him or her through public application, "thus informing him in an authoritative manner of what he is and what he must be" (p. 121).

Institutions that limit access to expectation and resource for those children who are *named* less capable or less important are *informing* the entire school of their identity and thus in all probability ensuring that the public negative identity remains stable. Moreover, such naming of potential permeates the sense of self. Bourdieu (1991) describes this as "telling the child what he is" (p. 52), instead of telling children what they might do and how they might do it. Social constructions of norms, values, and intentions toward individuals and groups are inevitably part of the naming process. A society with unresolved problems of prejudice and discrimination cannot help but integrate ramifications of such problems into construction of institutional classification systems. Silin (1995) thus argues that all categories applied to human beings can lead to unwarranted assumptions and, indeed, harmful bias.

"But wait a minute!"an experienced classroom teacher might reply, "we cannot pretend that all children come to school with the same background, readiness, and innate ability!" This is true. All children are constantly operating and progressing on different levels and in different ways. The harm in socially constructed classification does not lie within honest recognition of current progress; rather, it is embedded in unwarranted assumptions about permanency of human characteristics combined with stratification of resources and opportunities. Greene (1973) suggests that, while there will always be a wide range of social and intellectual differences, teachers must still question the criteria used for tracking and take a critical approach to any standards used to determine human worth in institutions. Rist (1970) further suggests that the success of educational institutions should be measured not by the treatment of high-achieving children but by the treatment of those children who do not achieve. "So long as the lower-status students are treated differently in both quality and quantity of education, there will exist an imperative for change" (p. 448).

Labeling, Bias, and Language

Chapter 5 of this book focuses on issues and problems inherent in deficit-based terminology applied to children. This section provides a brief overview of the problem of bias in all classification. Although one of the main functions of human language is stating facts about things and persons and events (Strawson, 1963), seemingly factual descriptions are contextual and emotive, and never simply true or false (Toulmin & Baier, 1963). Silin (1995) provides an example of the emotional and contextual nature of language through an examination of differential descriptions of people who have AIDS. In the early days of AIDS awareness, he points out, the media often changed labels and descriptions based on how the AIDS virus was contracted. People with hemophilia were "blameless victims," babies were "the most hapless victims," while gay people with AIDS were described with assumptions of moral wrongdoing (p. 16). Silin's personal experience confirmed the ways in which bias shaped the attitudes and language of many. He describes, for instance, a lover who is dying in the hospital of AIDS. A nurse who is engaged in difficult bedside treatment responds to the suffering of the patient by saying, "I am not responsible for you being here. You only have yourself to blame for that" (p. 37). Her words embody a judgment with inescapable ramifications for the way she cares about and treats her patient.

Giroux (1988a) provides yet another example of differential use of descriptive language. He points out that school students who actively resist alienating and oppressive school experiences are labeled deviant rather than resistant, because labeling them resistant would raise very different questions about the reasons for their problems. To indicate that a student is deviant is to imply that the school is a neutral force and that the problem lies within the individual.

On the other hand, to indicate that a student is resistant raises *inquiry* about treatment, resources, emotional experiences, quality of instruction, and possible discrimination within the school. Labels can shift blame or they can create a climate of responsible action.

Educators must not shortchange their own knowledge and intelligence by failing to recognize the subjective nature of interpretations of human ability, characteristics, and behavior. Likewise, they should abandon naive assumptions about the existence of neutrality in the way human problems and unfortunate social conditions are perceived and described in institutions. A wealthy and prestigious parent of a child diagnosed with a learning disability may receive empathy and support, while a single parent on public assistance may be blamed for a similar problem. A child from a family with high status may be excused for behavioral excesses for which a child from a housing project may be denigrated or excluded.

All socially constructed knowledge leading to systems of human classification should be open to inquiry and change. The complexity of human nature and the vastness of the human spirit deserve full recognition in any attempt to name the potential of individuals. Perhaps it would be helpful for educators to think of themselves as specially trained photographers capable of capturing an endless variety of perspectives, characteristics, abilities, and meaningful behaviors in their students. Their many conceptual snapshots, collected over time, are all useful in the process of education. The language that describes these snapshots can create new perspectives on human ability and enable the democratic ideals of equality and liberty to open continual opportunities for all students.

ACTIVITIES TO ENHANCE UNDERSTANDING

1. *Media analysis.* Newspapers and magazines are an excellent source of popular perceptions of current educational issues. Select several recent articles on public school issues such as school choice or educational standards. Read the articles and analyze the approach they take to the problems. Can you determine a presence or absence of democratic themes in the discussion of public education? Do you perceive an assumption that the public schools continue to be central to American goals, or do you perceive a lack of interest in and support of public schools? Do quotations or citations foster critical dialogue about the continued role of public schools in a democracy? Do any educators who are quoted make strong affirming statements about public education and professional accountability?

2. *Creating snapshots.* Select a partner or a small group with which to work. Ask your partner or one person in the group to describe a child in her class

or a child he knows in another context. (Tape-record this description or list the main characteristics described.) You or other members of the group should ask a variety of questions about the child (What does he like to do? What adult does she seem to relate to well?). When a full picture of the child has emerged, compare the original description with the present descriptive information. What information was included and left out at the outset? How could the emergent information help an educator to discuss the child in a positive manner?

4

Talking About Restructuring and School Reform: A Democratic Perspective for the Dialogue

The first three chapters of this book have focused on the internal language of education (the way educators themselves tend to talk) and the relationship of educational language to moral and democratic principles. This and the following two chapters will move outward in three different, although related, directions. This chapter will examine the current directions in reform and restructuring of public education, especially in terms of the public dialogue about specific school problems. Chapter 5 will focus on the historical educational problem of deficit terminology and its powerful influence on public dialogue about children. Chapter 6 will then move into an examination of areas of educational policy and leadership that can enhance the refocus of educational language. The three chapter topics ultimately connect in classroom practice as they all affect daily experiences of children and teachers. Although there is widespread engagement in dialogue about school reform, it is ultimately teachers who have the power to implement the intentions and desires of the profession and the democratic society as a whole.

FRAMING THE TROUBLE WITH SCHOOLS

Many Americans believe that our public schools are in serious trouble and they share a concern that what is happening in our public schools is fateful for our society as a whole. Hopefully, this concern can strengthen the sense of mission and community necessary to create schools that continue to liberate the human mind (Sarason, 1990). Our public schools, no matter how troubled at present, continue to have the power to help our diverse child population to construct alternative and better worlds (Smith, 1990). This power can be unleashed only if educators find ways to articulate a liberating and alternative vision to what is most deeply problematic in our current social and political environments.

Viewing Public School Problems as Democratic Problems

In a democratic society, problems in public education should become a lively format for political and social dialogue. The nature of public schooling inevitably embodies the complexities and inconsistencies of egalitarian goals positioned against capitalist competition. Because the state of democracy is always viewed more accurately as an aspiration than as an accomplishment, public dialogue about schooling in America can and should take the form of inquiry, public self-examination, and energetic regeneration of fundamental democratic principles. Public criticism of schools should be viewed as a threat only if it undermines democratic commitments to schools and children; public desire for school renewal is positive in a context of concern about the future of America and its children. Educators should be on guard, however, for indications that school criticism represents a troubling change of political direction away from commitments to equal rights and opportunities for all citizens.

Current Demands for Change

Educational change is everywhere, and teachers and schools in America and most of the industrialized world must deal with it more than ever before (Hargreaves, 1997a). The current focus on school reform is an extension of steady criticism extended toward educational institutions since World War II. American schools were considered too permissive in the 1950s and factory-like or irrelevant in the 1960s. Criticisms turned to failure to deliver the academic basics in the 1970s and blame for weakening the position of the nation in the world economy in the 1980s (Heslep, 1989). From the 1970s to the present time, this pervasive criticism of schools has created the impetus for a dizzying number of real and attempted alterations in the process of public education. Reforms have focused most strongly on academic content and higher standards for students and teachers (Elmore, 1990b). This overall process of change has fallen under the umbrella of restructuring and has been shaped by external public forces such as policy demands for standards-based reform, school–business partnerships, implementation of new technologies, several forms of school choice, subject-specific initiatives, and the self-desire of schools to seek improvement (Hargreaves, 1997a). Areas of restructuring have included curriculum and instruction, authority and decision making, new roles for school personnel, and accountability systems for teachers and students (Ellis & Fouts, 1994). There are a countless number of public and professional views about what schools need and how they should change.

What *does* the public think? To help answer that question, let us consider a survey by a doctoral student named Dale, who is taking an advanced seminar on school reform. As part of his seminar research, he has asked a wide variety of people, "What is wrong with our schools today?" Here are seven answers he received from the following individuals:

> A *relative:* "The teacher unions have ruined the schools. Teachers used to be dedicated individuals, and now they just punch a time clock. My wife works in a school cafeteria, and she says the teachers refuse to do anything extra for the kids."

> A *neighbor:* "I don't think they teach basic skills any more. We hire young people every day who lack simple abilities in reading and math. The kids are studying about drugs and AIDS and sex education but they do not seem to learn what is important for getting and holding a job."

> An *educator:* "It is much harder to teach today than it was 10 years ago. Families are much more dysfunctional now, and there were fewer standardized tests and curriculum demands in the past. More kids act really difficult in school, and neither the administrators nor the parents seem to know what to do about it."

> A *student:* "School is really boring. A lot of our teachers just hand out worksheets and tell us to be quiet. Some of our teachers are nice and funny, but some always seem to be in a bad mood. I don't think I am learning too much."

> An *administrator:* "The politics and the paperwork are really intense. I spend my day going to meetings and filling out forms. There are a lot more problems with children and parents than there used to be. We have parents who never show up, and parents who want to run the school. The teachers tend to be much more dissatisfied and I struggle with school morale."

> A *community leader:* "I don't think parents are aware of their responsibilities. For example, the kids need computers. The families tell me they don't have the money, but I see the kids wearing tennis shoes that cost well over $100. I don't think the parents understand the impor-

tance of turning off the television set and reading to their children. I talk about this in church constantly, but as a minister I do not have as much daily influence on families as I would wish."

A *school board member*: "The schools are inefficient and they are wasting money. When I look at the annual budget, items like busing kids and hiring substitute teachers seem staggering. We are cutting art and music from the curriculum but I cannot see what we are getting for that money except more red tape."

When Dale begins to draw and analyze themes from his research, he develops a much more comprehensive understanding of private perceptions of public education. Each individual he interviewed seemed to have a strong and critical view based on his or her own experience and interaction with schools. He now wonders how a more unified public response to the problems of public education might be encouraged.

ASSESSING AND RESPONDING TO CHANGE

As the above section indicates, disaffection with schools takes many simultaneous forms and directions. Many members of the public have not been in a school for many years, and yet they believe that they are in a good position to criticize schools. There is no doubt that it is a tremendous responsibility for educators to try to meet insistent (and not always pleasant) demands for change. Yet, it is important for them to continue to analyze criticisms and question the implications of suggested reforms for democratic commitments in public schooling. Will proposals of school choice, for example, strengthen or weaken structural commitments to equity for all students? Will partnerships with business expand or diminish the power of educators to provide equitable services to their students? Will new national or local standards improve or damage the access and opportunity of children who traditionally have been marginalized in schools? The answers to important questions must not be silenced in a blind rush to follow trends or respond to criticisms. Educators have the right to fully examine the ramifications of externally and internally driven changes and to articulate concerns about those ramifications. Any apparent disregard for democratic commitments to children, teachers, or schools should be actively confronted.

The tone of castigation and alarmed criticism that permeates the public call for improved schooling, and frustration at the intractability of many school problems, can distract both educators and the public from a democratic conversation. Statements indicating sentiments such as "American education is doing a mediocre job," or that even sustained periods of reform have resulted in "so little to show for our labors and our money" (Finn, 1992, p. xi), move the dialogue away from a sense of public community and mutual responsibility. What are Americans actually seeking in school reform, and what is and is not possible to achieve through school reform?

It is interesting to note that advocates for school change in the 1960s, many of whom based a conceptualization of schools as pathways to the remaking of society on their experiences in the civil rights movement, received little support from the business community. In contrast, it is the business community that led the call for school reform in the 1990s, with educators often resisting. The emphasis over the past 30 or more years appears to have shifted from social justice to economic survival.

While the involvement of business in public education is discussed later in this chapter, it is prudent at this point to question a business-driven approach to school reform that does not address the social transformations that extend far beyond the corporate world. Extensive and profound changes in economics and technological transmission of information, compounded with global spread of ecological danger, the geopolitical reconstruction of the global map, the reconstitution of cultural identities, and even redefinition of human selves, must all be central to educational dialogue (Hargreaves, 1994). Educators, who are, of course, trying to adjust to these changes in their own family and community lives, also must make constant shifts within their professional institutions. The demands they face, in union with children and families, far transcend the interests of the American business community.

Educators need to develop a language of response to calls for change based on human concern for children, families, and communities. This language can reiterate moral responsibility to protect the interests of democratic life in the ongoing process of school reform. No matter what current social changes are taking place, all citizens continue to need to lead daily lives requiring critical thought, rational communication, and productive relationships. Educators can stress the importance of democratic education in fostering not only academic skills but the attitudes and dispositions that form responsible members of society. In doing so, they can impose their own vision of school reform as a vehicle for protection of democratic ideals in the lives of all Americans.

Change in the Context of Democracy

In the face of an almost overwhelming amount of published literature on school restructuring, this is a good time to pause and measure the democratic directions of school change. Elmore (1990b) describes restructuring as a "garbage can" (p. 4) of fluid and unspecified perceptions of problems and solutions. I believe that educators must examine a confusing array of perceptions to find the most important issues upon which to focus.

The language of reform should be one of inquiry into fundamental assumptions about schools. For example, a common theme in school reform language is concern about the ways in which conservative and bureaucratic schools block changes required by an otherwise dynamic society (Ellis & Fouts, 1994). This is a real problem when one considers that public schools are functioning much as they did at the turn of the twentieth century. Yet, in truth, schools have attempted many dynamic changes, and many educators and their professional associations have enthusiastically engaged in efforts to meet the physical, emotional, intellectual, and spiritual demands of daily service to a highly challenged child population. Has the *major* barrier been bureaucracy and conservatism, or rather has it been the social, economic, and political inequities that undermine the process of school improvement? A dynamic public conversation about those inequities could give voice to frustrated concerns of educators who resist reforms they see as insincere or inadequate in light of the challenges they face with their students and in their school communities.

Any simplistic finger pointing that bypasses the serious ramifications of socioeconomic inequity will lead to specious and empty attempts at school reform. The educational profession, unlike many others (notably business), labors under the ponderous expectation of fairness, equal access, and equal outcomes in spite of gross differences in social and economic advantage. Children cannot help but bring the ramifications of widespread social dilemmas into the classroom, and teachers are expected to deal with those ramifications with far less support and fewer resources than they need in many cases. Impersonal and unfeeling demands for objective school improvements cannot do justice to what is most human and important about teaching and learning.

School reform conceptualized without heartfelt understanding of moral and human dimensions betrays the deepest callings of public education. Language of school reform that assigns easy blame and simplified solutions is distracting the American mind from important issues of social and economic justice. Authentic change in schools, just like real change in human beings, will require time committed to reasonably paced progress on unknown and sometimes unwieldy paths. Respect for the people involved, and understanding of the highly complex nature of systemic institutional development, is necessary. Educators cannot afford to be resistant or defensive, but they can take a proactive stance in focusing the dialogue of reform in positive and substantive directions.

Power and Conflict in Reform

Real school reform cannot take place without real assessment of power relations and power-related issues in education. Problems are always related to structures of power, and real challenges to existing power involve inevitable conflict and tension (Sarason, 1995). Efforts to restructure schools that do not alter fundamental aspects of the educational enterprise represent a form of "tinkering" (Ellis & Fouts, 1994). Without a common agenda that addresses real problems and takes the conditions of teaching and learning seriously (Elmore, 1990a), reformers will continue to focus on problems that seem manageable and gloss over important problems that are seen as too controversial (Sarason, 1995). The absence of conflict inevitably indicates that issues of power are being skirted or ignored. This creates a cosmetic but insubstantial context of change and in the long run undermines the good work and good will of many individuals.

In artificial climates of change, principals and teachers may spend hours meeting to establish priorities that subsequently are ignored in politically based funding decisions, or community stakeholders may be engaged in a series of hearings or committee meetings with foregone conclusions. Likewise, parent–community school councils may be created along with a silent directive to principals to keep the direction of discussion and change under careful control (perhaps directing parents into volunteer efforts to raise money for school computers rather than encouraging inquiry into current inequities in district designation of technology funds to individual schools). Efforts to change without a substantial shift in power lack integrity and soon exhaust even the most willing participants.

Conflict over Unbalanced Resources. A key power issue in school reform is that of equity. Heated conflict between those who have more than their equal share of school resources and those who have less is an inevitable though difficult aspect of real school reform. The current language of school reform often skirts inequities as well as the academic stratifications that rationalize their continuation. It promotes higher standards for teachers and students while saying little about "persistent inequality along race and social class lines as low-income students and students of color experience fewer resources and less powerful learning environments" (Oakes, Wells, Yonexawa, & Ray, 1997, p. 43). Policy that dictates change while failing to address real barriers to progress is artificial and harmful. Integrity in school reform requires the courage necessary to face conflict embedded in the issue of school resources and opportunity.

Educators, who hopefully can be leaders in the public conversation about fairness in distribution of resources, also must be prepared to address inequities in issues of tracking in schools. As long as any school-based stratification of students remains associated with overt differences in the amount and quality of school resources provided, it will be an inevitable component of conflict over resources. While some students and communities indeed are penalized by inequality and stratification, others benefit greatly. Nieto (1992) reminds us that there are always winners as well as losers in discriminatory school circumstances. When the winners are vocal and articulate parents from advantaged district neighborhoods, some or many of whom view their own professional status as superior to that of educators, the political controversy can be daunting.

Rather than demand actual resources, these parents may simply insist on retention of the existing unidimensional use of intelligence or standardized tests to assign unequal opportunities. This, they know, will maintain the superior position their children now enjoy. Educators may have a conflict of interest in public debates of equity issues if their own children are benefiting from placement in top school tracks, or when they are the friends or neighbors of those who demand continued tracking. These will be moral dilemmas with the potential to provide generous leadership so badly needed in a society where so many children face unequal treatment.

Naive, although idealistic, would-be reformers who assume that current winners in the distribution of educational resources will have a positive response to redistribution may be shocked by the anger and conflict in which they are quickly immersed. There is little in the literature on school change to prepare educators who are committed to equity for the more contentious aspects of reform (Oakes et al., 1997). Angry conflicts can escalate quickly and may involve personal castigation of those who suggest measures for increased equity. These conflicts also can bring to the surface many ways in which unfair, deficit-based assumptions about disenfranchised children are used to protect and preserve the status quo.

A Case of Gifted Education. Consider the example of a community conflict over a district program for children designated as gifted. A small but vocal parent advocacy group has discovered that, in their district of 15 elementary schools, only one school in the most advantaged area is receiving funds for a gifted program. When a few members of the group testify for more equitable distribution of gifted funds at a school board meeting, they are unexpectedly met with a large turnout of parents whose children are in the currently funded program. More than 20 of the parents testify in support of the program and warn the school board that they have the power and money to remove their children from the system and enter private schools if their special gifted resources are not continued. One parent says, "If you want the best children to remain in your schools, you are going to have to give them extra resources." Another parent asks, "Why water down our program to give our money to schools in which there are few or no real gifted children?" A third parent angrily states, "These less advantaged kids already have their special services and programs just to keep them on grade level. Our more intelligent children should have special services too." The members of the advocacy group feel overwhelmed and angry about the attitudes and behaviors they have encountered. As they leave the meeting, they notice most of the school board members talking in what seems to be a positive exchange with the parents from the gifted program. They overhear a comment that "next time they'll know better than to try to challenge the kind of parents who really care about their children's education."

Connecting Reform to Responsible Social Dialogue. As the above scenario indicates, it is most often a mistake to assume neutrality in the distribution of school resources and community responses to change. As professionals and citizens, committed educators are going to have to press reformers not only to address equity issues but to look outward to society to seek ways of restructuring fairness and access into the lives of all schoolchildren.

> Until and unless we find the political will to redistribute the wealth and soften the inequality growing like a cancer on our civic culture, we will have a society that is ever less civil and ever more divided into warring camps, regardless of how public education is reorganized or curriculum and instruction programs changed. (Molnar, 1997, p. 39)

Maintaining the Focus on Children

Children have neither voice nor power in the current debates over school reform. The dialogue on restructuring belongs to adults who speak in areas of policy, administration, politics, philosophy, and social criticism. How can educators be sure that children remain the focal point of meaningful educational change? The schools exist to serve the needs of children, and children will gain or lose the most from the changes that eventually are made. Educators who are most in touch with the daily lives of children—classroom teachers, university partners, school administrators, and others—have the knowledge and understanding necessary to build public caring about what happens to children in schools.

Who are the children? Generalizations about children so often fail to capture their remarkable qualities and individual characteristics. The language of educators must rise above the preponderance of deficit-laden generalizations about so many children to focus on the ways in which individuals are affected by educational change. Consider these examples.

> *Bernardo* attends a high school that just implemented a de-tracking program. Although his use of English is not as fluent as he would wish, for the first time since coming to America 5 years ago Bernardo is taking a science class with several top-achieving students. He has realized for the first time that it is acceptable to ask many questions in class, as those students seem to do. Bernardo is starting to study harder, be-

cause he admires and wants to imitate the more confident and success-ful students.

Lakesha lost both her parents in a drug-related car accident 2 years ago. The aunt with whom she lives decided, now that Lakesha is ready to enter school, to try to falsify her address so Lakesha could be regis-tered in the full-day kindergarten in the more affluent school in her district. Unsuccessful, the aunt was required to register Lakesha in the half-day program in her local school. While the full-day program has computers and takes one trip a month, the half-day program does not.

Carla has demonstrated an unusual interest in numbers and counting since toddlerhood. Her private preschool teachers commented on her love of mathematics, and she got a perfect score on her kindergarten readiness test for public school. Now in fifth grade, Carla attends a sub-urban school that has adopted an advanced science and math program for middle and high school. Carla has been selected to begin advanced classes ahead of time and is already hoping to apply to medical school.

It would be helpful for reformers to think about individual children, like those above, when visualizing changes in schools (Astuto, Clark, Read, McGree, & Fernandez, 1994). Real children are engaged in complicated and demanding lives and will respond in a wide variety of ways to any reform. Think of a child whose young single parent recently died of AIDS, a child who must adjust to removal from an abusive home and placement in foster care, a child whose mother has just lost her public assistance and health insurance, a child whose successful professional parents are too preoccupied to notice her growing depression, a child struggling with the pressures of family tradition to attend a prestigious university, a child who is pregnant, a child who feels overwhelmed by social pressures in his affluent community—all need to feel cared about in school before they can benefit from changes in curriculum, standards, testing, or any other reforms.

Educators who are experienced in trying to raise the voices and realities of children to public view, in order to create greater public compassion, know full well the barriers that are in place. Children do not vote, they do not control resources, and they cannot reward or even really thank those who make efforts on their behalf. Children who are not successful in school, who have special or troubling needs, or whose behavior creates difficulty for others have a particular need for valiant adult supporters—particularly when their families are not able to help them. It takes an optimistic form of persistent idealism to take up the voices of children, particularly when society so often seems uncaring. However, as Sarason (1995) reminds us:

Ideals are ideas about what should be; at the same time we know and regret that we will fall short of the mark. It is one thing to aim and fall short of the mark; it is inexcusable if knowing you will eventually fall short of the mark, you do not even take aim. (p. 149)

The possibilities of a democracy are most poignant and human in institutions that serve children. As fatigued or discouraged as their educators might become, children need the protection of a language of hope and enthusiasm—a language created by educators that permeates school and society.

BUILDING A DEMOCRATIC DIALOGUE
WITH BUSINESS AND COMMUNITY

Educational reform since the 1980s has inspired 30 national reports, most negative toward current efforts to educate American children. The 50 states have appointed nearly 300 task forces in search of educational excellence, focused mainly on mastery of academic basics and national economic concerns. Educators themselves have had limited access to educational summits and task force meetings; in fact, they sometimes are treated as intruders rather than central participants in educational debates. Yet I call for educators to shape and lead national conversations that are inclusive and that respect the power of well-directed dialogue to renew commitments to public education.

As Goodlad (1996) points out, we need to *talk* across all levels of government and all walks of life: in schools, on the job, in homes, and in many different kinds of public forums. Language is a powerful force in all education and constitutes public life when common and important problems are discussed with a focus on decision. Our talk should be about our own responsibilities and rights rather than on what others (government and politicians) should do. Spectatorship makes for thin moral discourse; democratic engagement requires a sense of personal action (Parker, 1996). If our responsible talk leads to the strengthening of public sentiment and resolve, political and governmental action is more likely to be responsive (and we are more likely to remain involved).

Talking with Business About Education

Educational reform has been heavily influenced by the recent involvement of American businesses—in fact, the term *restructuring* is borrowed from the business world (Ellis & Fouts, 1994). Berube (1994) identifies the participation of business in national education policy as the third movement in American public education, the first two being the progressive movement and the civil rights movement. "For its part," he writes, "the corporate sector took up school reform with messianic fervor. Concerned about America's economic decline, business leaders were convinced that school reform was a means to restore U.S. technological superiority and provide a capable workforce" (p. 93). Business-based talk and analogy are increasingly present in the dialogue of school reform, but the profoundly emotional aspects of teaching and learning cannot be pushed aside for concepts such as strategic planning, cognitive leadership, and organizational learning (Hargreaves, 1997b).

Nowhere is business-oriented language more evident than in discussion of school choice. Consider the following description:

> The current choice movement is a move toward providing for individual differences. It represents modest experimentation with a market approach to education. Markets are renowned for tolerating a myriad of variations in human behavior—debates over the future of America's public schools must center on student and parents wants. No one knows what or how much education anyone else should have. The concern of the educational establishment must be in satisfying the needs of its clients. (Reinhart & Lee, 1991, pp. 36–37)

Notably absent from the above quote is a democratic consideration of justice and equality, or recognition of the responsibility of social institutions to determine indispensable components of education for all citizens. Rather schools are discussed as business enterprises and are conceptualized in "rational, managerial, calculative and stereotypically masculine ways" (Hargreaves, 1997b, p. 13). The tone of this language should be called into question by educators because, as Hargreaves states, "schools are not businesses. Children are not products. Educators are not usually out to make a profit" (p. 22).

Good (1996), in an analysis of the National Education Summit of the Nation's Governors and Corporate Leaders in 1996, notes "a growing disregard for the American common public school" (p. 4). He contends that, while public schools remain central to democracy, there is a discernible disregard for the value of public schooling and an unwillingness to invest in its current status. For this reason, Good finds that policies currently generated by business leaders are incomplete, unsupported by educational research, and thus unlikely to be particularly effective. "All some companies want is a tough curriculum and computer technology. Businesses can't develop long-range plans for schools if they don't see that educating children is about more than a job" (Scherer, 1996, p. 50). The goals of reasonable competition and economic well-being are well linked to the mission of preparing children for meaningful and responsible work, but a focus on job skills alone is far too narrow. Mere instrumentalism designed to secure a profit for society should be superfluous in a democracy that protects the entitlement of each student to life, liberty, and the pursuit of happiness (Astuto et al., 1994).

Educators who are committed to the moral and democratic principles inherent in public schooling should seek redirection of critical aspects of dialogue and partnership with American businesses. Education is, after all, a powerful force in the total development of human beings on whom society will depend not only for economic stability but for meaningful civic involvement and strong family responsibility.

> Preparing the young to be good adult workers is only one of the purposes of schooling. . . . We also need better democrats, more people aware of the common good and willing to work for it. We need capital humans quite as much as human capital, narrowly defined. (Tyack, 1997, p. 23)

Future citizens are needed not only to participate in business but to inquire into the contribution of the business enterprise to the economic, political, and moral health of the nation.

> It has never been economics alone that defines America. If we choose as a culture to push back against the economic forces that would otherwise divide us, it is within our ability to do so. And the consequences of choosing otherwise . . . by pretending that the choice is not ours to make . . . is to cease being a society. (Mitchell, 1997, p. 5)

Educators can model responsible civic involvement by asking their own public questions about the best role of business in education and in society. For example, how does the fact that U.S. corporations seek tax breaks and subsidies in localities affect school resources? How does the fact that corporations increasingly reach out to skilled workers outside the United States and pay them a fraction of what they would be required to pay in America affect the job prospects of our students? (Berube, 1994). Businesses are playing a major role in school criticism without acknowledging the job crisis created not by a lack of student skills but by the transnational movement of jobs to countries with more docile labor and weaker environmental controls (Hargreaves, 1997b). Just one month after the governors/big business summit on education, a budget bill was signed into law that slashed Healthy Start funds from $104.2 million to $93 million while increasing military spending and continuing to subsidize the savings and loan crisis and bailout (Good, 1996). These issues may well have an impact on American children that is as long lasting as any educational experience.

A moral language of education should address the values as well as the power of American business. The common ground of service to the nation and commitment to human opportunity should be central to the discussion of preparation of future workers. In addition, educators should steadily assert that schools also play a critical role in preparing citizens who are committed to social justice and morally conscientious about the common good.

> The real challenge in connecting schools with the world of work . . . is not just to build partnerships with business, but to create partnerships that are morally defensible and educationally worthwhile (and to be sure they stay like that!). (Hargreaves, 1997b, p. 11)

The language of educators *should* be different from the language of those in business, and educators can position themselves strongly in the democratic commitments of what continues to be an essential human service profession.

Understanding Relationships with Families and Communities

The process of school reform and restructuring has focused not only on partnerships with businesses but on stronger relationships among school, family, and community. Educators tend to be in agreement that both schools and children benefit from home and community support, and indeed that schools suffer in the absence of citizen interest and parental responsibility. The actual design of the desired relationships with key players outside the school, however, is often amorphous. Sarason (1995) captures the particular problem of conceptualizing parent involvement in schools:

> It is quite fashionable to proclaim the necessity and desirability of parent involvement in our public schools. Such proclamations have the ring of virtue, inclusion, and a democratic ethos. If this affirmation of value and goal is well intentioned, the fact is that it is too often empty rhetoric and when it is not empty rhetoric, the actions they give rise to are more like shadow boxing or, less frequently but fatefully naive in the extreme about the problems they will engender. (p. 11)

Parent and community involvement implies a sharing of power, and thus potential conflict over issues of control in schooling. Educators should carefully articulate the changes that are sought and try to understand the effects of those changes on existing power structures. Without analysis and planning, efforts to engage families or communities in the process of public schooling may be little more than a hollow source of chaos or ultimate disillusionment. Partnerships that are "meaningful and moral" rather than "cosmetic and superficial" must reflect the desire to create an authentic dialogue about the most important goals (Hargreaves, 1997b, p. 11). The basis of authentic dialogue is a shared agreement that relationships create obligations, particularly relationships that surround the needs of children in families, communities, and schools. Sergiovanni (1992) poses the idea that schools, families, and communities that embrace a sense of responsibility to children can support one another in the creation of democratic ideals and the fulfillment of moral obligations.

While schools, families, and communities are interdependent, they each have different roles and obligations in the development and protection of the young. Lines of understanding drawn between the responsibilities of schools and families often are blurred in postmodern society, with resulting confusion and resentment in relationships (Elkind, 1997). Parents may express distrust or dissatisfaction with teachers; educators often feel that parents are not adequately fulfilling their role. Educators can lead the way to better relationships, even in this very difficult climate, by articulating the roles for which they hold themselves accountable while assisting families in developing a fuller understanding of their own responsibilities to school-age children.

Coleman and Churchill (1997) identify two major barriers to authentic family–school partnerships. The first is created by ambiguous definitions and the lack of a conceptual framework. Partnerships, they suggest, should always include themes such as educational modeling, advocacy, or empowerment. The second barrier is caused by diversity in the school–family environment, particularly when the perceived general level of parent education and socio-economic status is lower than that of school personnel. When cultural misunderstandings abound, parents may be viewed unfairly either as intrusive amateurs, apathetic participants, or hostile opponents. When frustrated, confused, or angry parents do create school problems, stereotypical assumptions unfortunately are reinforced (National Coalition of Advocates for Students, 1991).

Beliefs about parents can mirror unfair school systems of stratification. Advantaged parents in high-status professions may be seen as more caring and involved even when they rarely participate in school–community functions. Alternatively, less-advantaged parents, even when visibly involved in school groups and initiatives, may be viewed as more indifferent to their children. The language environment is as key to appropriate encouragement of parents and families as it is to children—generalizations and biased assumptions should be replaced by inquiry and sensitivity to diverse experiences and perceptions. Existing bias inevitably will be expressed in parent/community/school dialogue and will be an absolute barrier to moral, meaningful partnerships of those committed to the well-being of children.

Consider the experience of Mrs. Janas, who recently moved into her school district. Although formerly economically comfortable, she is recently divorced and temporarily reliant on public housing and public assistance to help her and her three children through difficult times. Attending her first Parent–School Committee meeting, as she did in her former school district, she is very offended at statements that are made. One of the teachers speaks critically of the families of the children in the lower track, apparently unaware that Mrs. Janas's youngest child is placed in the low track. When the teacher says, "Our lower children have parents who don't care enough to get involved," Mrs. Janas feels furious and then almost starts to cry. Later in the meeting, two parents suggest that the school should focus on "attracting the kinds of kids we want from better families, to offset the negative aspects of having so many children from the projects." Mrs. Janas is afraid to say anything because two of her children currently are having adjustment problems from the divorce and school change. She feels alienated and embarrassed, and decides that she will not return to another committee meeting.

The language of parent involvement must be inclusive and sensitive if it is going to be productive. Power can be as much of an issue in school/parent/community groups as in any other group, and some parents will participate in groups as a means of securing or protecting their children's resources. Issues of equity in tracking and grouping are very likely to emerge, as are other potentially controversial parent problems. The deceptive simplicity of school partnerships belies the problems of "vested interests understandably intent on maintaining the status quo, a lack of clarity (to be charitable) about means and ends, a surface appearance of unity and hope beneath which is confusion and anger" (Sarason, 1995, p. 15). Before educators openly embrace concepts such as site-based management, for example, they are well advised to anticipate loss of power, significant intrusion of a variety of outside interests, and significant changes in school governance and structure (Coleman & Churchill, 1997; Raywid, 1990).

The growing movement of parent opposition to what is viewed as the intrusion of schools into more personal areas of home and family responsibility also can create adversarial relationships. The Parental Rights and Responsibilities Act debated in Congress in 1996, for example, was directed at limiting the power of government bureaucracies, including schools, to interfere with the rights of parents to direct the upbringing of their children. Renewed efforts to create and pass similar legislation that potentially pits parents against schools should be anticipated (Willis, 1997). In addition to legislative initiatives, the burgeoning presence of school choice has the potential to create a climate of competition for resources that will deeply affect the relationships of schools, families, and communities. If the language of choice is not one of fairness and equity, our national sense of community in the nature and purpose of public schooling may be altered permanently.

The best partnerships with families and communities can emerge in an atmosphere of respect and mutual commitment to the potential of democracy to create a strong future for our children. Even in the spirit of democracy, however, power and control will continue to be central issues in the resolution of family/school/community conflicts. Schools as institutions are not immune to tendencies to retain the status quo of bureaucratic control. If those tendencies are dominant, they will foster avenues of family and community involvement characterized by artificial and manipulative formats for participation. Meaningful involvement may create new problems but also may meet the goal of helping schools to fulfill their most important purposes in our nation.

Innovations like choice, site-based management, and other forms of decentralization do create opportunities for partnerships. However, such innovations also could lead to troubling possibilities such as a sharp decrease in a sense of commitment to anyone's children or school other than one's own. Currently proposed parental rights legislation might enable parents to oppose efforts to implement curriculum that expands the acceptance or awareness of diversity, and thus call into question the democratic responsibility of public schools to prepare students for civic responsibility (Willis, 1997). Market conceptualizations of school choice might obscure the obligation of schools to seek excellence and equity for all students; school choice devoid of democratic commitments could place some marginalized families in the position of choosing inadequate and underfunded schools (Fennimore, 1996). If some parents and children are disenfranchised and cheated of rightful resources, so-called efforts to create family and civic involvement in public schools would amount to shameful pretense.

Insisting on Authenticity in Partnerships

Educators must not lose sight of the purpose of partnerships, which is to strengthen the power of schools to educate children as successfully as possible. Faced with the complexity and conflict of partnerships, educators are at risk of losing sight of their purpose and "allowing instrumental processes and procedures to become ends in themselves" (Sergiovanni, 1992, p. 5). Educators also will need to rise above the disappointments that emerge when participants in partnerships are neither benevolent nor committed to the interests of children (Hargreaves, 1997b). Authentic conversation, which often will be tense or troubled, will need to persistently weigh options against what is truly valuable for schools and children in the process of school reform (Mathews, 1996).

ACTIVITY TO ENHANCE UNDERSTANDING

Talk about school problems and school reform. Just about every person in America has ideas about public school reform. Often, these ideas fall into the category of "what is wrong with schools." Refer to the beginning of this chapter, where responses to the questions of a hypothetical doctoral student are discussed. Try this same activity, by asking at least five people, including a relative, a neighbor, an educator, a school administrator, and a community leader (e.g., minister, school board member) the following questions:

- What is wrong with public schools today?
- Who is at fault for existing problems?
- What areas of public schooling need to be changed?
- What should all children be entitled to in terms of public education?

When you analyze the responses, look for a sense of community and democratic commitment (or a lack thereof) to public education. The following questions can guide your responses:

- Are schools, teachers, and children blamed?
- Does equity emerge as an issue?
- Is there a civic sense of connection to the schools?
- Are families and communities viewed as also responsible?
- Do democratic concerns about public education emerge?

After analyzing the responses, compare your conclusions with those of others who did this activity. Discuss the ways in which the language of educators might help to create insight and to direct or redirect public impressions of the problems and goals of public education.

5

Breaking the Bonds of Deficit Terminology

Successful education for any child must be built on respect for her or his potential to develop into a promising and productive adult. The power of education is diminished drastically when perceptions of the challenges or diversities of childhood lead to presumptions of deficiency or unworthiness. Expectations that are lowered by deficit-based assumptions directly interfere with feelings of efficacy, respect, and hope on the part of many educators. It is thus incumbent upon all educators to consider ways in which they and their institutions currently might be hobbled by the historical tradition of labeling children (e.g., learning delayed or limited proficiency) and grouping them under stereotypical categories (i.e., disadvantaged or at risk). The bonds between educators and learners are made fragile by deficit-based assumptions about children, families, and communities. The potential benefits of any compensatory intervention in the process of education can be overpowered by the interference of labels indicating damage or deficiency in children.

THE PROBLEM OF DEFICIT LANGUAGE

This chapter will explore troubling educational trends that have been created by the strong traditions of deficit-based language about children. Such language often has emerged in the process of economic and political responses to social dilemmas or special human needs. While children targeted in the past certainly deserved empathetic and caring interventions, the accompanying language of deficiency had the power to alter their schooling experiences in very negative ways. Today, the long-standing tradition of deficit-based labeling has expanded to the point where large groups of children (even all the children in a school or community) might be referred to as "delayed" or "at risk" with neither accurate assessment nor adaptation of educational intervention.

How do negative descriptions affect educational attitudes and behaviors? Imagine for a moment that you are about to become the teacher of children who have been described in the following manner:

> For most socioeconomically disadvantaged children, . . . strengths do not outweigh weakness. By the time these children reach school, poverty has taken its toll. Their social learnings are limited and inappropriate to the expectations of the school; their perceptual, reasoning and communication skills are frequently very limited. They are likely to perform at levels below the national average on verbal and nonverbal tests. As they pass through school, the difference between their performance and the national average increases in what has been termed a "cumulative deficit." (Wesby-Gibson, 1969, p. 6)

The above quotation, which reflects typical descriptive language from the 1960s and 1970s, would be likely to develop or support deficit-based assumptions in the reader. Many of today's educators were thoroughly immersed in conceptualizations of cultural deficit during their professional preparation. Even relative newcomers to education and other human service fields have been deeply affected by traditional descriptions of children that authenticate images of deficiency. While the original intent of labeling or defining problems was often to set a path for remediation, few realized how damaging the words themselves could be. The problem is that

> *Saying* someone is inferior is largely how structures of status and differential treatment are demarcated and actualized. Words and images are how people are placed in hierarchies, how social stratification is made to seem inevitable and right, how feelings of inferiority and superiority are engendered. (MacKinnon, 1992, p. 31)

It is important to revisit the historical emergence of a language of cultural deficiency and to trace from it the continuing tendency to use deficit terminology in educational institutions. Such a revisitation leads to an understanding of the many overt and hidden ways in which widely promoted connections between diversity and deficiency served as past barriers to the advancement of civil rights in educational institutions. It also leads to greater critical insight into the ultimate emergence of suggestions of genetic inferiority in the recipients of compensatory services and policies in the 1960s and 1970s.

Historical research-based comparisons of Negro (terminology at the time) and White scores on intelligence tests enabled geneticist Jensen (1969, 1973) to raise questions about the ultimate usefulness of compensatory social policies. Because similar (and more widely accepted) questions re-emerged in the more recent book *The Bell Curve* (Herrnstein & Murray, 1994), it is clear that educators must still confront potential social and democratic problems created by any language of human deficiency. Such a confrontation might well articulate not only the fundamental responsibility of educators to assign equal value to all learners but a concern about the continuing use of scores on intelligence tests to frame social conceptualizations of human worth.

Revisiting the "Culturally Deprived" Child

Federal initiatives in compensatory educational programs during the 1960s, an outgrowth of the civil rights movement, were supported by social science research on the problems and deficiencies of children who experienced poverty in the United States. This research created a comprehensive public image of disadvantaged children as fundamentally different from, and inferior to, others. Subsequent professional images based on a "litany of deficits, handicaps, [and] pathologies" clouded the practitioners' recognition of the assets of individuals (Sarason, 1995, p. 40). The concept of child deprivation became an amorphous catch-all for assumed links between poverty and child deficit. The following description of cultural deprivation, which emerged from research funded by the federal government and several prestigious foundations, reflects the scientific tone that validated negative assumptions about children:

> First of all, cultural deprivation may be seen as a failure to provide an opportunity for infants and young children to have the experiences required for adequate development of these semiautonomous central processes demanded for acquiring skill in the use of linguistic and mathematical symbols and for the analysis of causal relationships. *The difference between the culturally deprived child and the culturally privileged is for children, analogous to the differences between cage-reared and pet-reared rats and dogs.* (Hunt, 1968, p. 323; emphasis added)

Poor children, often described as coming from slums, also were described as having intellective deficits, affective deficits, and difficulty in postponing immediate gratification, and as possessing a low achievement drive (Deutsch & Brown, 1967, Stendler-Lavatelli, 1968). These negative assumptions could be extended to what might be considered generalized and unfounded insults such as descriptions of mental blocks to self-improvement, lack of family unity, and likelihood of slipping into crime. The problems of poverty became linked to problems of morality: "These people develop their own value systems, which are displayed in their behavior. They need help if they are to acquire new value systems that correspond to those extant in the country" (Crowe, Murray, & Smythe, 1966, p. 2). Stemming from speculations on the lack of value systems, some writers of the period expanded into more creative descriptions of their assumptions of the quality of the lives of the poor. Crowded living conditions, for example, were described as limiting the growth of intelligence. Consider the following description:

In the third year, when the toddler . . . is prompted to ask such questions as "what's that?" his questions are typically met with "shut up." Seldom do such parents, who are preoccupied with the problems associated with their poverty or who are chronically in a state of disorganization and apathy, ask the child questions that will force him to use language. (Hunt, 1968, pp. 325–326)

Inappropriate language development was stressed as a component of cultural deficit, and Jensen (1968) went so far as to say that

Spoken language among the lower class is less like written language syntactically, grammatically, and in all-over sequential organization and logical progression . . . language in the lower class . . . consists of a relatively small repertoire of stereotyped phrases and expressions. (p. 118)

Social class assumptions were applied not only to the development of language in children but to generalized family interest in education. Reissman, in *The Culturally Deprived Child* (1962), wrote:

What does education mean to the culturally deprived? It is perhaps easier to state what it does not mean. First, it does not have the same meaning that it has for many middle-class Americans. There is practically no interest in knowledge for its own sake; quite the contrary, a pragmatic anti-intellectualism prevails. Nor is education seen as an opportunity for self expression, self realization, growth and the like; consequently, progressive approaches are opposed. (p. 12)

This negative description mirrors those of many other researchers and writers, whose construction of social images of culturally deprived children helped to shape the form and delivery of compensatory education programs. In retrospect, many questions should emerge about the *intentionality* of intensively negative descriptions of those designated to benefit the most from the momentum of the civil rights movement. Notably lacking from such descriptions were themes of democratic community, establishment of links between people who were poor and people like the researchers and their own families, sensitivity to the feelings of those described, and a willingness to place blame on social inequities rather than the individuals who were harmed by them. The language of cultural deficit created an undeniable *distance* between the children of the poor and children in the middle-class mainstream of America.

Many parents of children who received compensatory services were shocked or hurt subsequently by the ways those services were described in the media. Consider the example of Willa, who in 1963 was 20 years old and the mother of two young boys when the Head Start program began in her city. Recently deserted by her husband, she was informed through the social worker who was helping her to obtain job training that her children would be eligible for the program. Willa had been told that the program would provide a free, early education to prepare her children to be successful in public school. A few months after entering the program, her sons' Head Start center was featured on the evening news. Willa's excitement soon turned to anger and embarrassment as she watched the program. The announcer described her community as a "poverty-ridden slum" and described the program as "a way to raise the IQ scores of children whose intelligence had been limited by parental neglect." As one of her sons and some of his friends appeared on the screen, the announcer went on to say that "these children have limited speech patterns, poor impulse control, and are likely to fall way behind other children by the end of first grade."

Willa still remembers her fury when she approached her children's director the next day. She and all her siblings had done well in school, and she constantly read to her children and encouraged them to talk and think. The director encouraged Willa to remain concerned about the prejudiced remarks she had heard on the news show, and invited her to become part of the parent board. Willa's subsequent activism in Head Start helped motivate her to finish a teaching degree in college, and she has been an elementary school teacher for the past 25 years. As a teacher she has worked hard to support the efforts of all parents to be aware of bias in schools and to help their children to be academically successful.

Racism and Scores on Intelligence Tests

The construction of cultural deficiency was reinforced by the validation of scores on intelligence tests as indicators of success or failure in compensatory education. As Jensen (1973) described this, "The main factor involved in scholastic ability is intelligence, as measured by IQ tests, and so the aims of compensatory programs have usually been described and assessed in terms of raising the IQ" (p. 11). Intelligence thus remained a word and image that ultimately created and reinforced current perceptions of social hierarchy (MacKinnon, 1992). By the time compensatory programs had been developed in the 1960s, over 382 studies had already been done on "Negroes," whom Jensen (1969) described as "disproportionately represented among groups identified as culturally or educationally disadvantaged" (p. 81). Studies of cultural deprivation became intermixed with ongoing racial research, a stated aim of which was to account for the "observed differential in intelligence test scores between Negro and white samples" (Deutsch & Brown, 1967, p. 306). Even after widespread criticism of the racial implications of his research, Jensen (1973) reasserted that "in accounting for the causes of differences among persons in IQ, the genes outweigh the effects of environment 2 to 1" (p. 397).

It is important to ask retrospective questions about the reasons why differences in IQ scores between racial groups were an important component of social science research on compensatory solutions to political, social, and economic inequities during the 1960s and 1970s. Why did a focus on possible genetic inferiority of individuals overshadow equal consideration of their resilience in the face of daunting social and political inequities? One could argue that a predictable end result of a search for scientific proof of inferiority in any group would be justification of existing social stratification as a fault of individuals, not society. Had the intention been to fortify and defend any disenfranchised group, one would have expected far more examination of the moral deficiencies of a society in which so much damaging inequity and discrimination continued to exist.

THE IMPACT OF DEFICIT LANGUAGE
ON COMPENSATORY EDUCATION

It is very difficult to develop a positive image of any person who has been described as deficient. Imagine, for example, a person who, having met a prospective marriage partner, poses a discrete inquiry about him or her to a mutual friend. If that friend responded that "s/he has limited verbal ability, poor motivation, familial tendencies toward criminality, poor impulse control, inability to delay gratification, low intelligence, and a highly disorganized social experience," the prospective relationship almost certainly would be abandoned! The unattractive description would far outweigh the inclination to explore unknown possibilities. Yet, when confronted with equally detailed negative descriptions of many of the children in their classrooms, American teachers somehow were expected to respond in a positive manner. In spite of the fact that "experience falls victim to the seduction of language" (Staten, 1984, p. 43), educators were presumed capable of forming high expectations for children described as distinctly damaged and inferior at the outset of the educational endeavor.

Many educators currently in the field were deeply affected by the deficit-based description of learners to which they were exposed during their college years. As a hypothetical example, Bruce has undergone many transformations in his 30 years as an educator. Now a principal, his undergraduate preparation took place in the 1960s. Bruce recalls watching the March on Washington on television while still in high school, and remembers how defensive and troubled his parents were about Dr. King's speech. Inspired by the emergent civil rights movement, Bruce attended a college with a strong teacher preparation program in urban education. Looking back, he is highly aware of the ways in which deficit terminology and a model of cultural deficiency permeated his college education. "Most of my White male professors presented the picture of the urban child as pathetic and needy," he recalls, "and we definitely were prepared to expect nonverbal and nonintelligent children. I remember my first year of teaching, when I was so amazed at the warmth and creativity of my children. Many of my parents were so caring and articulate."

Bruce now realizes that his assumptions about his students were often demeaning, and he often reflects on things he might have done differently as a new teacher. His attitude has been deeply affected by the multicultural education movement. Bruce first resisted multiculturalism, because it ran counter to his lifelong beliefs about the importance of developing one American identity. However, as he became more willing to examine the premises of his own personal and professional life, Bruce appreciated the opportunity to revisit civil rights concepts and reapproach efforts to become an educator committed to social justice.

Perceived Failures of Compensatory Programs

There is little doubt that compensatory educational programs made an immediate and continued difference in the lives of children. The proud history of the enduring Head Start program, for example, was built on the tireless efforts of many determined and talented professionals. It was the tyranny of the importance of the IQ score, so often central to program assessment, that had the power to undermine the public perception of the accomplishments of educational interventions. Unrealistic expectations that a child's score on an IQ test could rise significantly after short intervention, and unwillingness to give equal weight to long-term social, emotional, physical, and family gains, sometimes fueled pronouncements that compensatory programs were not successful.

Most notable in such negative assessments was *The Impact of Head Start*, a study conducted by the Westinghouse Learning Corporation in 1969. Based on research into 104 Head Start Centers, the report cited weak gains that tended to evaporate in the later public school experience (Berube, 1994). Following the publication of the study, Jensen (1969) declared that compensatory education, sanctioned by social science-based deprivation hypotheses, had been tried and had failed. Unfortunately, the language of deficiency and focus on scores on intelligence tests that had characterized compensatory intervention were used ultimately by some to unravel the perception of its usefulness.

Voices of Concern About Deficit Terminology

There were educators who openly challenged remedial programs based on hastily conceived models of child deficiency. Hamlin, Mukerji, and Yonemura (1967) wrote, for example, that

> The dynamics of the problems of discrimination, desegregation, integration and civil rights are not only extremely complex but changing at a very rapid rate. When we look honestly at the civil rights movement in the last few years, we are forced to reexamine some of the cliches that have become familiar in describing minority groups and socioeconomic classes. (pp. 6–7)

Other educators recognized the role of IQ scores in fostering continuing racial segregation and warned that "educators need to be doubly alert that the schools are not utilizing grouping practices which assist in maintaining and promoting social and racial biases" (Goldberg, Passow, & Justman, 1966, p. 10). Some educators were aware of the too-rapid development of compensatory services, which was based more on the immediately available funds than on knowledge that ultimately could be integrated into the fabric of education (Goldberg, 1967). Without a full development of intent informed by substantial research findings, such programs had the power to compound disadvantage, reinforce old prejudices, and "give renewed popularity to the now more dormant concepts of inherent inadequacy" (Gordon, 1968, pp. 405–406).

There was a strong critical response, in particular, to Jensen's (1969) article questioning the ability of compensatory programs to boost IQ and standardized achievement test scores. Angry charges of racism and disrespect for culturally different children laid the groundwork for the emergence of multicultural education and created an ongoing national forum on ways in which diversity should be incorporated into social science research agendas. Valentine (1971) captured the responses of many others: "Any theory of class or racial deficits of biological origin is quite undemonstrable, indeed scientifically untestable, in an ethnically plural . . . society" (p. 138).

A growing awareness of the internal problems created by theories of cultural deficits emerged in the literature related to compensatory education. Some researchers pointed out, for example, that the Head Start program had been based on a social pathology model of intelligence and behavior. They called for movement away from deficits in children back into a much-needed examination of the role of racism, classism, prejudice, and discrimination in later school failure. It is quite sad, in retrospect, to think that deficit-based terminology such as *poor impulse control* or *inability to delay gratification* really described the normal reactions of children who were hungry or unfamiliar with commonly interesting objects such as commercial toys. While disadvantaged children were described with such deficiencies, reprehensible adult indulgence in discriminatory behavior that justified unequal distribution of resources remained largely unexplored. Assumption of deficiency in children often was used as a rationale to set them apart from others. Compensatory programs thus may have, in effect, "emerged as an expedient alternative to school integration" (Chazan, 1973, p. 2).

It is important for educators to confront the damage done to children through the proliferation of deficit terminology:

> As we think today of child abuse, we must not exclude these acts of labeling for they are often more gross and insidious than overt physical acts of abuse, because they cripple the minds and spirits of families, children, and professional practitioners alike. . . . You know the following terms: "dyslexia," "Head Start," "minimal brain dysfunction," "culturally deprived," "restricted language code," "broken home," "single parent families," "readiness," "educationally handicapped," "multicultural," and "inner city," . . . certainly these activities and labels, in many if not most cases, have really represented a silent assault on millions of Black, Brown and poor children. (Hilliard, 1976, p. 16)

Such a history of deficit terminology in compensatory education must illuminate current efforts to refocus educational language, as it provides good reason to question the benefit of the association of deficit terminology with remedial interventions. A viable alternative is the establishment of socially responsible programs for young children justified largely by a language of concern for human development. While educational programs should address childhood harm and suffering caused by discrimination and poverty, and should project reasonable outcomes, their rationale should not be based on a litany of the deficiencies and negative characteristics of children to be served.

The construction of positive language is admittedly more difficult when funding sources require the labeling of program recipients. However, even when establishment of difficulties or disabilities is required, the strongest language surrounding the program can still focus on moral regard for and democratic commitment to humane services for their own sake. In the absence of such language, the forces of prejudice can continue to infiltrate the intentions and outcomes of any educational intervention.

Equity Versus Meritocracy

There has been intense public and professional conversation since the 1960s about the ways in which human differences in American people should be defined and addressed. This conversation is never neutral; it is always charged with personal and political interest. Because of continued social stratification along lines of race and class, the language of human difference ultimately constructs or strengthens one of two paths: (1) an opening of greater understanding and opportunity for people with diverse backgrounds, capabilities, and interests, or (2) justification of present stratification and access through focus on innate abilities and merits of individuals. Educators thus must be constantly aware of the direction and use of their own language about human differences, knowing that it has the power to either open or close doors for their students.

Those who wish to defend the neutrality of institutions and their policies tend to focus on the ways in which individuals do or do not deserve access to the best available resources and opportunities. As demonstrated in the discussion of compensatory education, the use of tests is one way to imply neutrality and fairness. Jensen (1973) indicated his belief, for example, that test scores tended to be validated by life performance.

Jensen focused on the competitive nature of social life and used a 1905 quotation from Edward Thorndike to emphasize his own beliefs about genes and accomplishment: "In the actual race of life, which is not to get ahead, but to get ahead of somebody else, the chief determining factor is heredity" (p. 28). Reflection on these comments should make it clear that educators need to analyze and carefully articulate the relationship of tests, individual worth, human potential, and fair access to resources.

Meritocratic theories have long reinforced presumptions of neutrality in schools. This presumption would indicate that resources are there for all takers and that ability alone determines who will rise and fall within the institution. When resources are unevenly distributed, however, meritocracies tend to create the aura of a contest between their constituencies (Brantlinger, 1993). Such a contest, when characterized by unexamined inequity, racism, and stratification, has predictable and discriminatory results. Subsequent professional and political interpretation of lower test scores unfortunately can be used to defend the status quo and blame the victim. A famous example of such interpretation is the statement of the Boston school board member who said, "We have no inferior education in our schools. What we have been getting is an inferior type of student" (Kozol, 1967, p. 199).

Advocates for fairness and equity have long recognized the need to question presumptions of meritocracy. Edmonds (1979), for example, stated, "Schools teach those they think they must and when they think they needn't they don't. That fact has nothing to do with social science, except that children of social scientists are among those whom schools feel compelled to teach effectively" (p. 16). Any time the language of difference becomes a language of stratification, the danger indeed exists that educators will begin to excuse themselves from accountability to positive outcomes for all children.

CONFRONTING THE BONDS OF DEFICIT TERMINOLOGY

The issues and debates surrounding compensatory education in the 1960s remain unresolved on many levels. A new language of education thus must actively confront the legacy of cultural deficiency and the continuing use of deficit terminology to protect the social, economic, and political status quo in America.

"At Risk"—A New Model of Cultural Deficiency?

The legacy of historical assumptions about cultural deficit may be most obviously present in the newer term *at risk*. That label was applied originally to students *who might be in danger of future school and social problems without adequate intervention*. In a sense, the term *at risk* was designed to save children with certain differences, experiences, or characteristics from the assignment of more permanent labels through instigation of early supportive services. In truth, however, it may now have become a substitution for older deficit models with parallel funding categories (Banks, 1995b). Bernard (1993) warns, "Labeling students 'at risk' can set in motion a vicious self-fulfilling prophecy. No matter how well-meaning, targeted programs that label children 'at risk' may be doing children more harm than good" (p. 47).

It is time to recognize that any educational discourse concerning child deficit may interfere with the sense of community necessary for greater movement toward social justice for targeted children. As Fine (1993) describes this problem:

> The cultural construction of a group defined through a discourse of risk represents a quite partial image, typically strengthening those institutions and groups that have carved out, severed, denied connection to, and then promised to "save" those who will probably remain "at risk." (p. 91)

Educational language should seek a clear path away from ongoing labels of risk, because such labels are perpetuating historical problems. Language must welcome all children into the educational community and inspire the professional and public imagination of what each child might become (Smith, 1990).

I believe that it is time to take definitive steps toward releasing American children from a stranglehold of stifling norms and categories of pathology (Weber, 1984). Deficit language places educators at risk for prejudiced behavior, which leads to avoidable failure in students (Postman & Weingartner, 1969). Knowing this, it is inexcusable to not take action. Likewise, the dynamic of racism, "given all the damage it has done, and its persistence and adaptability across time and space" (MacKinnon, 1992, p. 63), should be confronted whenever it emerges.

Such confrontation, however, is more difficult because the language of racism has become more subtle and interwoven with seemingly benign institutional practices. "If the racist act seems part of ordinary everyday procedure, not chargeable to this or that individual, it is highly effective" (Weinberg, 1990,

p. xiii). If racism and other forms of discrimination can infiltrate the process of education, so can a moral language with a focus on human agency and dignity. To stand against existing powers that reinforce assumptions of race or class superiority, however, educational language must be shaped with a fully grounded determination to create change in descriptive language about all students.

Taking Responsibility for Change

The use of deficit terminology is unlikely to disappear quickly or easily. Its use is deeply entrenched in educational tradition and is frequently reinforced when sources that fund special services require labeling. Systematic habits of thinking and speaking are hard to change, and some educators will resist those changes. The more closely changes in educational language are linked to restructuring of systems of stratification, the more resistance, both overt and covert, should be anticipated.

I want to emphasize that there is a difference between labeling for knowledge and organization and labeling with a harmful implication of deficiency.

> Labeling is a normal, useful cognitive attribute. To be opposed to labeling is like being opposed to breathing. Like so many attributes it can have untoward uses and consequences. Nowhere is this more clear than when we use labels in ways that divert our attention to people's deficits, downplaying or even totally ignoring their assets. (Sarason, 1995, p. 45)

It is educational language that focuses on deficit to the exclusion of asset, disproportionately applied to some groups of children more than others, that is a primary target for change. Many problems that do require diagnosis and remediation do not require automatic, permanent labeling. Public disclosure all too often creates distance or damage, which is why so many adults with potentially embarrassing problems go to such great lengths to keep them private.

Think back to Chapter 1, which stressed the importance of perspective reinforced by *sensitivity, accountability, and inquiry*. Statements that would be terribly hurtful or obviously unfair if made about one's own child, which cast unnecessary blame and diminish professional responsibility, which imply hopelessness, or which fail to pose and consider possible solutions, constitute inappropriate professional language. In terms of educational research and policy, blanket descriptions that reinforce negative public perceptions of groups or strengthen discriminatory resistance to equity or social change must be replaced with a balance of inquiry and respect for those being discussed.

Teachers bear a special responsibility for eliminating the use of deficit terminology in everyday school practice. "Wait a minute!" an understandably frustrated teacher might reply. "Now we have to examine every single word we say?" It is important, in response to such concern, that the refocus of educational language not be framed as one more addition to a steady stream of exhausting responsibilities. Rather, language should be viewed as a daily force that permeates all professional activities and is thus central to the life of teachers and students. The commitment to equal treatment of students, insofar as it is created and upheld by humane and moral democratic speech, should be the underpinning of every school-based relationship.

A refocused language of education need not contain an artificial pretense that differences do not exist among children. School activities are often competitive, and some children will perform on higher levels than others at any given time. Educators naturally will recognize and commend excellence in school performance but "must . . . also examine [their] roles in enabling certain students' goal attainment while neglecting others. Leaving low-income students' future in the realm of the unmentionable is certainly not an equitable practice for public schools" (Brantlinger, 1993, p. 189). Any teaching language that writes students off and provides justification for refusal to offer opportunities must of necessity raise moral questions that must be addressed.

Language and Multiculturalism

Multicultural education, which emerged during the civil rights movement of the 1960s and 1970s (Banks, 1995b), increasingly has constructed focused opposition to cultural deficit models and "ethnocentrism of methodologies and theories which do not give credence to the cognitive and intellective skills of the child" (Baratz & Baratz, 1970, p. 29). Multicultural education supports expansive affirmation of diversity as a desired attribute of a democratic society as it upholds respect for common humanity as the hope of the world society (Irwin, 1973). As multicultural education has continued to develop as a rich discipline, it has focused on issues of social justice and equity central to democratic values. Banks (1995b) explains that

> A major goal of multicultural education, as stated by specialists in the field, is to reform the school and other educational institutions so that students from diverse racial, ethnic and social-class groups will experience educational equity. (p. 3)

Hoffman (1996) notes that, in spite of profuse efforts, little is truly known about how to "do multiculturalism" in schools. Trivialized infusion of content or brief celebrations of certain groups can take place in classrooms where many children remain marginalized by a deficit-based construction of their families, life experiences, and intellectual abilities. All children, particularly those who experience discrimination, need a rich multicultural pedagogy that empowers them to understand themselves in relation to others, to challenge stereotypical perceptions of their culture and ability, and to participate in the naming of their own interests and intellectual desires. Only those educators who are committed to the liberation of marginalized children from the confines of deficit-based perceptions are able to design and implement such a curriculum.

In the absence of that commitment, resistance to true application of multicultural ideals often remains. This resistance can result not only in continued use of historical deficit-based constructions, but in application of new stereotypes that may emerge in the guise of multiculturalism. A poorly structured teachers' workshop on the learning styles of the geocultural group of children who attend a resegregated school, for example, inadvertently can reinforce lowered expectations and the subsequent absence of challenging academic curriculum ("Our children are action-based, right-brain thinkers who cannot respond well to structured academic tasks").

Multiculturalism that celebrates self-identity as it also frees children from stereotypes concerning the groups to which they belong, can open many possibilities for disenfranchised children. Integral to positive multiculturalism is concentration on a refocused language of education. During collaboration on the construction of a language of multicultural pedagogy that deeply challenges deficit-based constructions of human ability, educators can move beyond simplistic multicultural applications to "make further connections, connections that address directly the political and moral nature of the work needed to achieve a democratic society" (Cuffaro, 1995, p. 107).

Consider the efforts of the eighth-grade team of teachers in a large urban middle school to implement a multicultural curriculum. For many years, this integrated middle school has had a policy of creating heterogeneous classes in sixth and seventh grades but of tracking based on standardized test scores in eighth grade. The teachers have noticed for years that the tracking results in an almost all-White high track in eighth grade (White children are the minority in the school) and two nearly all-Black lower tracks. The teachers believe that this separation causes children in the lower tracks to lose self-esteem, to increase resistant misbehaviors, and to lose contact with many high-achieving role models the year before they begin high school. Furthermore, the teachers are concerned that the high-track students lose contact with diverse peers, that any existing tendencies they have toward negative racial attitudes may be reinforced, and that the opportunity for cooperation with diverse peers is lost.

Last year, the teachers petitioned the superintendent and school board to eliminate this tracking for a trial year, and also created a multicultural curriculum to be implemented in eighth grade. Called "Hands Across Our School and Communities," the curriculum includes community history research projects, community action projects, a school action project, and weekly seminars to discuss issues of difference and diversity. Intended to infuse all subjects, the curriculum encourages critical pedagogy that helps students to question and challenge the ways in which their schooling has made them think about themselves and their ability to succeed in school. Students complete each project in different cooperative groups. In addition, students are placed in study groups that match more advanced students with those who can benefit from high-achieving role models. Because a fairly large group of parents of students who would have been in the high track have raised questions about the new system of grouping, the teachers have created a series of workshops for interested parents in conflict resolution and diversity issues that may affect their children in later high school years.

Initiatives like the one described above are enhanced by a strong awareness of the use of descriptive language about students. Every educator undoubtedly encounters some remnants of deficit-based terminology or models of cultural deficit in daily practice. Such encounters provide a constant opportunity for activism and advocacy. Every act of countering negative and discriminatory terminology, including the creation of a liberating pedagogy for students, helps to redirect educational professionals onto a path of language focused on human possibility.

ACTIVITIES TO ENHANCE UNDERSTANDING

1. *Bias journal.* Designate a period of time (at least 4 weeks) when you can be particularly attuned to any biased statements made by those around you. Maintain a daily journal in which you note comments about diverse people made in your presence by colleagues, peers, professors (if you are a student), relatives, or even passers-by. If you are an educator or a student, you should have the opportunity to observe the language that surrounds you pertaining to ability, grouping, and relevant forms of diversity. If you are not currently in an educational setting, you can still observe the language of all with whom you come into contact.

   At the end of your designated time period, analyze your observations to identify themes. What major issues emerged, and how might you as a concerned individual support others in the refocus of biased conversation?

2. *Interviews of educators.* Locate two or more educators who experienced undergraduate preparation in the late 1960s or early 1970s. Ask them to recall the images of culturally deprived children to which they were exposed. What kind of field experiences did they have, and how were the skills and behaviors of their students interpreted? Have they changed the way they think and talk about less-advantaged children? Why or why not?

6

Leadership, Policy, and Teacher Preparation: Setting a Course for Refocused Language

Abraham Lincoln once stated that education was the most important subject in which people could be engaged (Fehrenbacher, 1989). Such a sentiment sheds a positive light on the fact that so many Americans are participating in what amounts to a national debate about the future of schools. It is worth repeating here that close attention must be paid to the central constructs of this public dialogue. Selfish or shortsighted interests can obscure or even silence democratic concerns, particularly if the voices of educators themselves are disorganized or weak. Educational leaders must establish their own vision, constructed with commonly held beliefs and commitments, and infuse it deep into the heart of the public conversation (Sergiovanni, 1992). Moreover, those who educate teachers need to emphasize the elements of democracy, equity, and social justice that will empower progressive school reform.

Such a vision should articulate passion for improvement, acceptance of responsibility for contributing to change, and a firm focus on the potential of all children. The bonds of deficit terminology, so detrimental to children, also can harm the ability of educators to articulate their own sense of efficacy. Why should the public have confidence in educators who appear to presume failure in a large number of students? The language of educational leadership thus should neither reflect nor tolerate prejudiced, unfeeling, overgeneralized, stratified, or hopeless talk about the children, teachers, and schools of our nation.

LANGUAGE, LEADERSHIP, AND EDUCATIONAL POLICY

Policy forces in education have been shaped since the 1980s by a language of reform. In response to 30 national reports on education, most negative, 50 states appointed nearly 300 task forces in search of educational excellence (Reinhart & Lee, 1991). Focus on reform consistently has reinforced a language of efficiency (back-to-basics) or economics (preparation for employment to support the business interests of the nation). The Clinton presidency responded to the theme of reform with three major legislative initiatives: (1) Goals 2000: Educate America Act, (2) a reauthorization of the Elementary and Secondary Act (Improving America's Schools Act of 1994), and (3) the School-to-Work Opportunities Act (Smith & Scoll, 1995). These and many other policy initiatives indicate the strong presence of government concern about schools.

It is undeniably important for Americans to be concerned about the national quality of education for all children. In these challenging times, schools still provide one of our final and greatest hopes for resolving a crisis of community across much of the developed world (Hargreaves, 1997b). The public dialogue about education must be substantial enough, however, to create meaningful change—change that will last and that can rectify the inequities that lie at the heart of so many educational problems of children.

A responsibly constructed language of educational leadership can temper unrealistic demands for a quick fix to school problems. The slowness and difficulty that have characterized educational change are likely to persist, so educators must help the public to see the good in complicated processes of reaching long-term goals. Much of the current language of school reform has been generated by noneducators whose interests and experience may be far removed from classrooms, and thus they fail to address the complex nature of educational change. It is up to educational leaders to persistently remind all would-be reformers that most successful change eventually must be implemented by one teacher in a classroom with 30 or more children. Respect for the real pace of child and adult development must be interjected into artificial and impractical suggestions for reform.

Many voices have been raised in the interest of educational reform, but only some have been heard. Tyack and Cuban (1995) state that "although many groups have entered school politics, especially in the protest movements of the past half-century, the apparent pluralism is misleading" (p. 8). Disproportionate authority over educational reform, they claim, has been held by policy elites, or people who managed the economy, who had privileged access to the media and to political officials, or who controlled foundations. However, educational leaders in city and state superintendencies, as well as members of school boards and representatives of teachers, also have had a recognized voice in school reform (Elmore & Furhman, 1995).

Some educational leaders who hold powerful positions in the reform process may have been drawn into adopting the language of business or politics—two fields that are increasingly characterized by short-term solutions to problems. It is far preferable, although admittedly much more difficult, for educators to temper the language of business and politics with reminders of the moral and ethical mandates of schooling in a democratic society. Consistent articulation of the responsibilities of schools to meet complex and demanding human needs can redirect public attention to the realities of children and teachers. It also can shape a better public understanding of the real time and effort required for significant change in educational institutions.

The Realities of School Change

In a society that promotes intensive competition and that values immediate success, the language of leadership must carefully frame the complex problems that require persistent long-term efforts to resolve. Sustained and meaningful progress inevitably will include successes and failures, particularly when the American child population is experiencing a wide variety of stresses outside of the schools. Sincere efforts have failed for many past reasons, including poor conceptualization of problems, inappropriate rate and breadth of change, too few resources, a notable absence of long-term commitment, opposition of parents, or isolation of the focus of change from important structures of schooling. Those who lead changes may be ineffective, overcontrolling, or satisfied to use the early success of innovations to move on to higher personal ambitions (Hargreaves, 1997b). Many of these failures have been highly instructive and have enabled courageous educators to redesign their efforts and renew their focus on change that really works. The public and educators alike must continue to anticipate continued challenges in school reform, simply because of the unpredictable nature of human and institutional development.

Although the dialogue of reform is focused most often on schools and educators, it is important not to lose sight of the fact that educational reforms are "intrinsically political in origin" (Tyack & Cuban, 1995, p. 8). The politics of education are centered squarely in the concerns of adults, many of whom have personal ambitions and long-term career goals at stake. Pressures can be in place that strongly discourage efforts to address the most difficult problems because of risks to reputation or advancement. There are no quick and neat solutions to the manifestation in real classrooms of the serious problems of poverty, family disintegration, or community violence. That is why a refocused language of educational leadership must remain firmly focused on the daily concerns of children, teachers, and families—as well as the democratic interests of our nation. Artificial and empty politics consisting mainly of telling exhausted teachers what more they should be doing for challenged and troubled

students, without acknowledging the larger social, political, and economic challenges in their way, will continue to do more harm than good. Real change
must involve difficult questions, professional risk, social discomfort, and persistence when failure does occur.

Most school problems have developed over time and have come to involve
a variety of complicated issues. For example, consider the case of Mona, the
recently assigned principal of an urban middle school. Although the superintendent told her that the district values the involvement of parents and community
in education, he also warned her that the former principal had very serious
problems with parents who were critical of the school. The superintendent
gave Mona a copy of a book called *Business Suggestions for School Management*.
In the chapter on managing parents, the book made three suggestions: (1)
solve conflicts quickly, (2) keep discussion focused on specific and appropriate
concerns, and (3) redirect complaints into productive activities.

Soon after the school year begins, Mona is aware of very strong conflict
between parents and staff. Parents complain that teachers are inaccessible and
disrespectful toward them. Teachers complain that parents who are not meeting
their own responsibilities to their children make too many demands on the
school. The assistant principal tells her that the former principal had refused
to acknowledge the extent of the problem and blocked any potential discussion
of the conflict at Parent Teacher Organization (PTO) meetings. He also had
tried to engage more vocal parents in fund raising to purchase computers for
the school.

When Mona raises the problems with parents at a faculty meeting, many
angry feelings about families and community emerge. The union representative
reminds her of contractual limitations on required contact with parents, and
the teachers are generally unreceptive to the idea of a parent–teacher task
force. Several parents call her to enlarge on criticism and complaint about the
school, but they also decline an invitation to serve on a task force. Mona soon
realizes the risks and potential failure of her efforts to resolve these problems,
but also believes that it is important to take responsibility for addressing real
and complicated problems within the school. As an insider, she has a real
understanding of the time and limitations of the change she will undertake.

The above example highlights the complexity of change when serious
problems have developed over a number of years. Oversimplified recommenda-
tions or demands for quick and easy solutions can only stand in the way of
leaders with the courage to tackle some of the intractable and long-standing
educational problems that exist today.

Power to Impose Terms

Educators who have the greatest access to the process of school reform
have more responsibility to impose definitive and moral meaning onto the

identified terms of school change. "The power to define such terms is a linguistic marker of relationships among players in the policy process" (Placier, 1993, p. 382). Business clearly has held a position of power in the development of linguistic markers; thus key terms such as *restructure, standards*, and *excellence* have been interwoven into the discussion of school reform. When the terms are put together, the message seems to be *the American power elite is concerned about having well-prepared workers to protect its interests in the global economy; schools therefore need to have higher standards so students achieve higher test scores as markers of their future competence.*

It is up to educational leaders to impose terms of *equity, fairness*, and *social justice* onto the school reform debate. Critics of schools too often are allowed to leave unexamined the problems of their own professional environments as well as the economic, political, and social inequities that are heavily straining the schools. Hopefully the message to go forward will be that *the American education elite is concerned about the preparation of future citizens who have experienced the benefits of a just democracy during their school years; thus society and all its sectors must be held accountable to high standards of contribution to the well-being of school and community.* When teachers, parents, and community members witness educational leaders with the courage to examine social and political truths, and to hold other sectors accountable for the same, their faith in the ultimate value of a national conversation about education can be renewed. The sincerity of a language of leadership that refuses to ignore their daily struggles will support ongoing efforts to create meaningful change.

REFOCUSING THE LANGUAGE OF TESTING

The language of school reform has almost become synonymous with a language of testing and standards. On the surface, it can appear logical to identify an objective means for ensuring that schools and students are meeting the expectations of society. Beneath the surface, however, the determined focus on testing, to the exclusion of other equally important concerns, should be questioned. Recall for a moment the discussion in Chapter 5 of IQ testing as it related to evaluation of compensatory educational programs. Although the civil rights movement had raised significant social and political issues that were closely related to the formation of those programs, a language of democratic concerns for children fell silent in many ways to the language of testing. In today's climate of reform, we see again a pattern of focus on tests to the frequent exclusion of conversation about the democratic and moral purposes of schools. The absence of that conversation, along with a historical link between test scores and expectations and resources, raises old concerns about the uses of assessment to retain current social stratification.

It appears that standardized testing of children provides a comfort zone that allows leaders and policy makers to approach surface problems without addressing underlying questions of educational quality and purpose. While appropriate standards and tests do provide important information, and are one tangible measure of school and student performance, they are never a sole indicator of the conditions and quality of schooling. As long as the resources of schooling are so vastly different for diverse groups of children, standardized tests can be far more a reflector of the results of inequity than of the real potential and actual gains of many students.

If educational leaders will accept a lesson from history, this would indeed appear a timely moment to take command of the language of reform and move it firmly from testing to more comprehensive considerations. Standardized tests are often *not* the best indicator of child progress and teacher effectiveness, and they do not evaluate the presence or absence of social justice in institutions. Educational leaders can help the public to extend its perception of assessment to consideration of the ways in which schools do or do not prepare students to participate in the democratic interests of the commonwealth. They also can challenge all reformers to address the real social and economic conditions of schools—conditions with strong impact on testing outcomes.

Addressing the Connection of Reform and Testing

The entrance of testing into the language of the power elite, according to Corbett and Wilson (1991), has caused the role of measurement of student achievement and competency to undergo a fundamental change "from being tools that local educators use to diagnose student weakness to being policy instruments that state politicians and officials use to compare schools and districts . . . and encourage reform at the local level" (p. 13). To evaluate educational initiatives, these authors suggest, states have adopted one method of operation, which can be best characterized as "reform by comparison, with standardized tests as the key component of the strategy" (p. 2).

Many school superintendents undoubtedly have been coopted or coerced into adopting the language of testing. Some reasons for this are the expectation of hiring committees that prospective superintendents will give assurances that test scores will rise under their leadership, the fact that state governments may provide incentives to districts that raise scores, and that the politics of individual communities may revolve around analysis and comparison of standardized test scores in individual schools. The professional ambitions of superintendents will be enhanced by a quick rise in standardized scores—a form of career capital to be cashed in for stronger public relations and a more competitive stance for future professional positions.

This entire process often leads to pressure-filled accountability measures for teachers, designed to ensure that they make high test scores a classroom priority. Ultimately children themselves are pressured to score well on tests and may spend hours in school rehearsing on dittos or worksheets that replicate standardized assessments. Children whose development has been delayed or harmed by difficult life circumstances, or those with diverse patterns of learning and behavior, may well have lower test scores. However, rehearsal for tests interferes with other rich and deep learning activities that would be far more likely to help them catch up with their peers. For example, a child who is not reading on grade level is much more likely to benefit from a variety of meaningful reading experiences than from hours practicing for reading tests. Many advantaged children, whose test scores may be high, also might lack skills in problem solving and critical thinking. Children who are disadvantaged or delayed but resilient, who are making enormous social, emotional, and cognitive gains in school, may have low test scores that belie their hard work and progress. There are also concerns about equity and standardized testing, which will be discussed in the following section.

Excessive focus on tests and scores indicates a fall into the area that I call *simple public talk*. This talk distracts citizens and leaders from difficult conversation about the deeper dimensions of reform. Whether simple talk be about testing, or the length of the school day, or the number of preparation hours allotted to teachers in schools, or the salaries of educators—it fails to raise the public questions that can truly move schools ahead. "No program for blueprint for future action can be given until the American people become aware that education can be used for either liberation or social enslavement and that education is not good in and of itself" (Spring, 1976, p. 266). Educational leaders can be seduced away from moral questions and problems in education by a "managerial mystique" that places "process before substance and form before function" (Sergiovanni, 1992, p. 4). Committed educational leaders with substantial participation in policy debates can help the public realize that high test scores alone cannot end the present ferment in education (Burrup, Brimley, & Garfield, 1988). Democratic and moral issues concerning social justice, equity, and the purpose of schooling undoubtedly will remain.

Testing and Program Development

The tradition of policy-driven testing in response to educational concerns is long-standing. To address and reshape this tradition, educational language will need to lead to better conceptualization of the role of standardized assessment in the development and evaluation of state and federally funded interventions. Discussion should take place at the point of program development about the accountability of a democratic society to provide services for children and the wide variety of ways in which those services strengthen society as a whole.

Assessment can be designated as *inquiry* into the progress both of children and the many social institutions that support them. The simple policy talk of testing should not be allowed to obscure the complexity of changing children *in* school when intractable inequities exist outside its doors. Also, children cannot make significant progress if the fact that they receive funded services places them in a school climate characterized by negative labels or disparaging assumptions. The problem of public identification and labeling also should be fully discussed at the point of development and implementation of state and federal initiatives.

Finally, even excellent compensatory programs cannot by themselves overcome damage done by negative social forces, economic injustice, or institutional racism. The progress of children requires a public commitment to excellent educational opportunities for all, and special supports for those who are known to be specially challenged. It also requires acknowledgment that institutions need to improve and that prejudice and inequity must be confronted continually by society at large. Thus the language of educational leadership must both defend the concept of democratic commitment to appropriate educational services for all children and challenge society to address the underlying causes of many educational problems.

The Example of Title I. The Title I program of the 1964 Elementary and Secondary Education Act (ESEA) provides a historical (and current) model of problems that are created by the interrelationship of compensatory programs, deficit terminology, and the language of standardized testing. Legislation that funded this program was passed at the height of national attention to civil rights and social reform, and was influenced by the popular conceptualization of the culturally deprived child. Senator Robert Kennedy insisted on a strong evaluation component at the point of Title I development because, as he said, "I have seen enough school districts where there has been a lack of imagination, lack of initiative, and lack of interest in the problems of deprived children . . . my feeling is that even if we put money into those school districts, then it will be wasted" (Peterson, 1983, p. 97).

The above chain of events should have a ring of familiarity to today's educators. First a widespread social injustice comes to public attention, and then education is targeted for resolution of the problem. Following this, children who are targeted for intervention are labeled with deficit terminology. Then policy makers who distrust the intentions of teachers and schools call for the inclusion of stringent testing demands as a way of forcing districts to use the funds appropriately. (Educators should wonder if their own use of deficit language about children in schools contributed to the impression that hope and creativity were not present for less-advantaged children.) Ultimately, the democratic conversation about the original social injustice is subsumed into concern about test results, and the children who were targeted for help can become the ultimate victims—first of negative labeling, and then of derogatory assumptions created by their continued inability to score well on standardized tests.

The entitlement programs created by Title I left the existing structures of the schools themselves unexamined and unchallenged: "The add-on approach derived from the assumption that children at risk are deficient and did not address the concept that schools are inadequate to meet their needs" (Bastian et al., 1985, p. 80). The Title I pull-out programs often focused on mastering low-level skills and included intensive multiple-choice and norm-referenced tests (Smith & Scoll, 1995), which made it hard for schools to be creative with funding. In some ways, entitlement programs became new mechanisms for "stigmatizing and segregating children, generating a new bottom tier in schooling for the masses" (Bastian et al., 1985, p. 81). The danger of doing further harm to targeted children was created by what Peterson (1983) referred to as the large and worrisome unintended side effects of labeling students.

Polakow (1993) suggests that compensatory interventions actually were designed as a pedagogy of the poor, which needed to denigrate the conditions and abilities of children in order to justify the spending of the taxpayer's money:

> A pedagogy of the poor ensures that poor children have no entitlement . . . they must be classified for eligibility. They experience their *other* status in the kind of programs they have access to, and their lives become commodities to be priced in terms of worthwhile investments. For, after all, we are serving these children at taxpayer expense. We educate them to contain them so they do not endanger our privileges. We compensate them for what their families have failed to give them, not for what we have taken away from them. (p. 130)

The recently reauthorized ESEA continues to provide a significant infusion of economic resources into schools and has addressed some of the past criticisms of Title I. However, given the long tradition of deficit terminology, it is realistic to expect that public labeling of children who are disadvantaged will continue to have unintended negative effects. In fact, the very use of the words *Title I* ("Over 50% of our population in this school qualifies for Title I services.") or *Head Start* ("Almost the whole kindergarten class is Head Start kids.") may be synonymous in some settings with the words *at risk* or *culturally deprived*. I argue that it is up to educational leaders and policy makers to insist on *rights without labels*—policies that entitle all American children to an appropriate education. This should be viewed not as special compensatory service for a few, made necessary by their own failures, but as part of our continued national journey toward equal opportunities for all citizens.

An Example of Changing Terminology. Educators who seek funding for programs may need to change their habitual use of deficit conceptualizations as a rationale for need. Consider the example of two separate groups of educators from two public schools with a similar student population who are applying for local funding to provide a voluntary afternoon homework support program. The first group has expressed the need for the grant in this way:

> The children in our school are at risk for a variety of reasons. Many come from single-parent families on public assistance, while others live in foster care due to abusive or neglectful homes. Over 60% of our students are below grade average in reading. This program will help children to complete their homework with the guidance of a qualified tutor. Without the program, many children will return to disorganized homes where there is little support for school success.

The second group has expressed the need for the grant in this way:

> The educators in our school believe that all children benefit from an extended day in which support services for homework are provided by experienced tutors. Our students represent a wide span of diversity in terms of family formation and income, and many of our parents are employed on a full-time basis and thus return home in the early evening. All students will be welcome in our program, and the service will be designed to support cooperative work and peer tutoring. The students will range from those who have low to high achievement scores and those with a variety of special needs. Every child will have the opportunity to complete homework and also to assist peers in approaching assigned tasks.

The first group may feel that it is necessary to compile a deficit-laden image of children in order to receive the grant. The second may trust that the funder will respect their view of all children as deserving of support and intervention—and of the opportunity to help and work with one another as equals. In each example, the language used will ultimately have an effect on the social perception and acceptance of the students.

REFOCUSING THE LANGUAGE OF STANDARDS

Standards, like testing, have a logical place in the process of education. Most would agree that it is good for educators and students alike to aspire to sound and appropriate markers of achievement. Standards that are *imposed,* however, may be less useful than standards that are set by those most affected by teaching and learning in educational institutions. This is particularly the case when standards are created by those who do not understand the process of change in human development and behavior.

It is often necessary for educators to assert their own power and their own critical resistance to standards that do not reflect what is most important or desirable in the education of children (Giroux, 1988b). Educational language must strike a delicate balance between acknowledgment of real problems in schools and resistance to standards that do not address the most important issues facing schools. Cookson (1995) attempts to strike such a balance:

> This is not to say that American education is as successful as it should be. And no one questions the reality that public schools in the inner-city are a national scandal and an affront to a basic sense of decency. One wonders, however, whether simply legislating standards will lead to substantial improvement in these schools without an infusion of resources and the development of an educational ethos that stresses democratic values as national goals. (p. 415)

There is a vast difference between meaningful standards and scores on tests. *What Matters Most: Teaching for America's Future* explains that "standards that reflect . . . imperatives for student learning are largely absent in our nation today. That is not well understood, however, because American students are at once overtested and underassessed" (National Commission on Teaching and America's Future, 1996, p. 25). If the public is to be helped to differentiate between meaningful assessment and standardized testing, it is again up to educators to form a language that reflects deeper conceptualizations of the measurement of true learning. Part of this important task is to move away from viewing numerical scores as a form of competition between groups of students. Rather, educational language should focus more strongly on many forms of assessment as ways of understanding what students know and how to better help them to improve skills and reach full potential. As Green (1983) describes this:

> Educational excellence is present whenever and wherever there are those activities that nurture the capacities of the mind that we share as humans. . . . In its pursuit we do not ask whether those participating will end up with equal status in the eyes of other human beings. (p. 340)

Intrinsic to many discussions of testing and standards is the scapegoating of educators for the real and perceived failures of American education. Few would deny that improvements are needed, or that there are indeed educators (among the many who have been exemplary in practice) who do not represent the best of the profession. However, all educators have been under tremendous pressure to respond to social changes and to meet the needs of children who are experiencing considerable stress in family and community. Fairness requires, at the very least, that the same level of accountability expected of educators be expected of families, communities, and society at large. When accountability outside of the school is lacking, then educators deserve far more empathy and support for the complex responsibilities they undertake on a daily basis.

I believe that any discussion of standards should reflect respect for children, for educators, and for the ways in which human experience and development intersect with the process of intellectual growth. If standards are set *first* for adequate resources, humane treatment, and relevant pedagogy for all students, positive and productive learning outcomes are far more likely to follow. The language of standards should be firmly set in a dialogue of caring about a high-quality education for every American child.

TALKING ABOUT TEACHER EDUCATION

Teachers are the crucial link between policy and practice, and their performance is the most telling application of the effectiveness of all (researchers, professors, administrators) who work within the profession of education. The choice of a career in teaching, however, leads neither to high status nor exceptional financial gain. The Report of the National Commission on Teaching and America's Future (1996) states that "teaching continues to be treated as low status work . . . in the United States, teaching has long been viewed as little more than a combination of glorified baby-sitting and high-level clerical work" (p. 14). It follows that teacher education on the university level also lacks prestige when compared with other majors, and in fact Goodlad's 1990 study "revealed that teacher education suffered from low prestige and low status, an unclear mission and identity, faculty disquietude, an ill defined body of study, and program incoherence" (Ladson-Billings, 1995, p. 748).

Lee Shulman (1983) describes American teachers as the most highly trained in the world, even though they enter the field with far less training than in any other profession. Given the fact that only one-sixth of the typical 4-year undergraduate program in teacher education is devoted to pedagogical subjects, expectations of expertise should not be high. As Schulman points out, "What is truly amazing is the frequency with which outstanding instruction is accomplished by teachers who have been provided so little training and supervised practice before being thrust into responsibilities of a mature professional" (p. 491). As undergraduate and graduate programs continue to wrestle with these ongoing problems, they have the opportunity to examine and revitalize the language of teacher education. How can teachers best be prepared to meet the demanding challenges they will face in their future classrooms?

The Limitations of Teacher Preparation

It should be clear that any student entering a career in teaching now must be prepared for practice in a climate of intensive reform and change. Yet, internal and external talk to the contrary, many schools of education remain constructed to support the status quo. Professors and researchers may write about change and reform, but the structure of their university practice and curriculum appears to assume that existing structures of schools will and should continue (Sarason, 1996). Thus, standard teacher preparation programs stress subject competence and pedagogical skills, and utilize traditional field placements that essentially require that student teachers comply with the status quo of the schools in which they are placed. Professors may urge students to utilize creative techniques in their future classrooms, "but traditional lecture and recitation still dominates in much of higher education, where faculty do not practice what they preach" (National Commission on Teaching and America's Future, 1996, p. 32). In addition to utilizing traditional teaching methods, education faculty may hesitate to challenge the status quo in their own university or in the field placements of their students. They thus fail, I believe, to model the risks and rewards of moral inquiry into school practice for their students. Because of limitations in teacher education, many undergraduates continue to graduate prepared only to replicate the current conditions of teaching and learning in schools.

Consider the example of a student named Dolores, who is completing her junior-year field experience in an urban elementary school. Her university methods courses, taken in conjunction with the placement, focused on traditional lesson and unit plans. Dolores was required by her college professor to teach a unit on butterflies, prepared as part of university coursework, during the field experience. Her supervising classroom teacher, however, saw the unit as an extraneous imposition on his own curriculum. He thus suggested that she "just play the game" and teach the unit only if her college supervisor appeared. Otherwise, he suggested, she could just sit in the back of the room and observe.

When the supervisor did come, near the end of the placement, Dolores taught one of her prepared lessons on butterflies. After the lesson, she privately discussed several dilemmas with her professor. In addition to discouraging her efforts to fulfill university responsibilities, her supervising teacher also had made disparaging racial remarks about several of the students. Dolores, who was bilingual, was particularly upset about the negative way her teacher treated several non-English speaking students. When she offered to work with them, he said, "No need to bother, because they are exempt from the standardized tests."

Her university supervisor was sympathetic but advised her to remain silent so she could get a high grade and a good recommendation. When Dolores later confided her confusion and disappointment about the experience to a relative who had been a teacher for many years, she was advised to go along with her supervisors, stay out of school politics, and then try to get a suburban teaching job after graduation.

The overt and covert language of teacher education to which Dolores was exposed did not allow her to "deeply understand and handle real problems of practice" (National Commission on Teaching and America's Future, 1996, p. 32). Rather, she was encouraged to meet requirements that lacked sensibility and was discouraged from reflective interaction with her mentors and students. Her response to the fact that her concerns about the ethical dimensions of the classroom were silenced was, not unpredictably, to decide to seek out a job that she assumed would not present her with such troubling moral dilemmas.

Teaching for Social Reconstruction

A refocused language of teacher education must reflect the responsibility of the teacher to take part in the democratic debate of the purpose of schooling. As Soder (1996) writes:

> If teachers are in large part political agents, if teaching is at heart a moral and political endeavor and only secondarily a matter of technique or subject matter or teaching to the text, then there are significant implications for how teachers need to be prepared. (pp. 246–247)

New teachers, with rare exceptions, will be confronted almost immediately with the essentially political issues of stratification, distribution of resources, deficit assumptions about some students, and low expectations for some students' success. They also will need to deal quickly with the dichotomy of district curriculum standards and pressure for high test scores, and their own interest in creative and individualized curriculum. The ability of new teachers to transcend barriers and frustrations, and to impose their own values and beliefs on the choices they make daily in classrooms, will depend to a great degree on the quality of preparation they received.

If that preparation involved opportunities for self-reflection, critical thinking, and analysis of multiple dimensions of teaching in real classrooms, new teachers are better able to approach their problems with a sense of personal responsibility and moral agency. If, instead, their preparation was focused on replication of the status quo, they simply may be subsumed into the existing ethos of the school and accept unequal resources, unfair stratification, or stultifying curriculum as inevitable. In the process of that acceptance, much of their own passion and vision may be lost.

Preparation for Moral Choices. If future teachers are to be enabled to take a moral and democratic stance in the public schools of America, their preparation must allow them to confront and articulate the dilemmas they observe. This will require insightful mentoring from professors who help them develop a balancing act between several different skills—cooperation with colleagues and supervisors in schools, collaboration with parents and communities, demonstration of effective teaching skills, and expression of moral agency by engaging in the process of school reform.

> To alter a system that is deeply dysfunctional, the system needs teachers who regard teaching as a political activity and embrace social change as part of the job . . . teachers who enter the profession not expecting to carry on business as usual but prepared to join other educators and parents in major reforms. (Cochran-Smith, 1995, p. 494)

Successful teacher preparation programs need to be constructed upon commitment to activism as well as to excellence in pedagogical practice. Multicultural courses that explore the deeper issues of diversity and oppression can support a commitment to activism, as long as they provide substantive insight into the conflict that arises in schools when bias or inequality is openly addressed. Insubstantial approaches to multiculturalism, characterized by surface exploration of cultures or artificial jargon about appreciating diversity, do little or nothing to help teachers when they are faced with serious engagement in the issues of racism, sexism, and other forms of oppression (Ladson-Billings, 1995).

Whether courses focus on methods, subject competence, or diversity, they must in some way delve deeply into the serious moral issues faced daily by educators. Examples and case studies of those whose moral agency allows them to be change agents in the midst of complex problems should be explored. Also, field experiences should allow students to reflect upon and question practice, to develop multiple perspectives on problems and solutions, and to take positions in conflicting situations. An honest and critical dialogue between students in education and their professors and school-based mentors must persist in opening doors to inquiry throughout the teacher preparation process.

The Example of a Constructivist Field Experience. If institutions that train teachers are committed to supporting constructionist professional growth,

I believe that conventional field experiences must be redesigned. Students should have the opportunity to confront real and important problems, and to learn to talk and think about them in honest, positive ways. For example, Gable University, located in a rural area, has a professional development school in the local district. The school principal, three lead teachers, and three professors from the university have collaborated for the past 5 years to train prospective teachers. An understanding existed from the outset that the school was experiencing some difficulties in funding, racial tensions between two long-standing factions in the community, and ramifications of extreme poverty of some of the children. It was agreed that student interns would be given the opportunity to reflect on the real dilemmas of the school and that all supervising faculty would support their professional development in the process.

All student interns, participating university faculty, and supervising teachers sign a yearly *pledge of commitment and confidentiality.* The pledge was created to shape a professional climate that encouraged deep discussion of problems with an understanding that an ethic of confidentiality was expected at all times. Each student intern completes a case study and a curriculum study during the field experience. The case study allows the intern to select one child for observation, interview, and tutoring. The curriculum study provides the opportunity for development of a long-term project that integrates areas of the curriculum and needs of diverse students. A weekly seminar gives students and mentors the chance for in-depth conversation about problems, barriers, successes, and application of learning to future career goals. A special focus of the seminar is the development of ways of talking about problems without using negative criticism or deficit terminology—rather, inquiry is used to gain insight and direct future intentions for teaching.

Students in constructivist field experiences like the one above are not pressured to be silent about the inconsistencies they see between the ideals of the academy and the realities within the school. Rather, they can be fully engaged in reflection on dilemmas and struggles that they are likely to confront throughout their teaching careers.

Accepting the Challenge. Teacher educators are irreplaceable role models, as are classroom teachers and school administrators. The current focus on professional development schools is promising (Valli, Cooper, & Frankes, 1997). Whether in professional development schools or more traditional field placements for student teachers, however, prospective teachers must have the opportunity to think critically and compose alternative structures of thought about what they observe. Says Cochran-Smith (1995):

> Teacher educators can perhaps best handle the tension between the lesson plan stance and a transformative, inquiring stance on teaching by arming their student

teachers with thorough knowledge on current practice as well as the ability to construct and act on a trenchant critique of that practice. (p. 521)

In addition to balancing reconstructivist and traditional methods for teacher preparation, those who prepare teachers must model a language of responsible reflection on practice. Collaboration between universities and schools in which student teachers are placed also must encourage confrontation of habitual use of deficit terminology or discriminatory stratification of students. There are risks when teacher educators and prospective teachers maintain an honest conversation about school practice. Acceptance of those risks, however, is intrinsic to the construction of teacher preparation that truly provides significant opportunity for reflection and development of long-term insight.

Including Teacher Unionism in Teacher Preparation

It is curious that responsible participation in one's future union is so often absent from the formal coursework of teacher preparation. Although they are undergoing challenge and transformation, the American Federation of Teachers and the National Education Association continue to play very important roles in teacher practice and educational policy. It often may come as a surprise to new teachers that contractual issues are fundamental to their professional experience in schools. They may discover a union-related mind-set in some of their colleagues, which has a definite impact on the language environment of the school. Of course, some new teachers who choose employment in private or other alternative schools will be less directly affected by union issues. But all teachers are affected by the public perception of widespread teacher unionization in America.

A Case of Contractual Job Issues. New teachers may be unprepared for criticism from some colleagues if they choose to go beyond contractual requirements in fulfilling their job responsibilities. Consider the case of Jamaal, who is a first-year teacher in a small suburban school. Somewhat surprised that almost all the teachers leave with the children at the end of the day, Jamaal enjoys staying for a few hours to ready his classroom for the next day. However, a small group of teachers has approached him various times to suggest that he follow the contract and leave by 3:30 p.m. Jamaal continues to stay, but senses dislike and disapproval from some of the teachers who have approached him. When during a faculty meeting the principal asks for volunteers to join a parent–community council, several teachers indicate interest as long as the meetings take place during the school day. Jamaal raises the issue of parents who are employed during the day and suggests evening meetings. He is visited later in the day by a teacher who informs him that evening meeting attendance is not a part of the official job description, and suggests that he reconsider his position.

Jamaal talks the situation over with his assigned mentor, an experienced teacher in the school. The mentor supports Jamaal's dedication to his job and concern about parents, but indicates that contractual issues will always be central to the structure and design of teacher responsibilities. Jamaal, he says, will need to make his own decisions but also be mindful of the fact that some in the school may be uncomfortable with his willingness to volunteer time.

Many teachers, whether novice or experienced, have at times to balance their own sense of what needs to be done with the provisions of their union contract. Case studies during teacher preparation can help students to think through issues like volunteering time for school projects, calling parents in the evening, attending weekend professional development seminars, and other important activities that may be neither compensated for nor required in their job descriptions.

Unionism and Professionalism. "A profession," according to former AFT president Albert Shanker, "describes someone who is an expert in his or her field and who thus requires little or no supervision because he/she has a high degree of decision making power" (Mungazi, 1995, p. 91). Teachers often are not considered professionals both because they tend to be heavily supervised and because their decision-making power tends to be limited in the school setting. The fact that teachers belong to unions also creates significant questions about their professional status (Kerchner & Mitchell, 1988). Collective bargaining often plays an important role the process of school restructuring, yet it is bounded by many restraints (Streshly & De Mitchell, 1994).

There is a strong public perception that the due process rights created by unions block the ability of school districts to address issues of teacher incompetence. Albert Shanker did agree that although due process rights were a necessary protection for teachers who questioned the administrations or policies of their school districts, they also made it too difficult to fire unfit teachers (Checkley, 1996). The public suspicion that teacher unionism is self-serving has been reinforced when teachers, increasingly demoralized by job stress and public criticism, have mobilized on their own behalf only when threats to job or salary were imminent. "Far too many teachers assume their union should meet their needs because they pay their dues; they do not see the relationship between the union's ability to meet their needs and their active support or involvement in the union" (Romanish, 1991, p. 116). Stronger teacher activism in addressing the democratic concerns of schools, a potential answer to the teachers' union dilemma, could utilize a union-based language of teacher accountability. This in turn would likely have a very positive effect on the public perceptions of teachers, their unions, and schools.

The challenge of the perception of teachers' unions should be seen as an intrinsic component of policy and leadership in education. While unions must protect teachers from exploitation, they also can help teachers who are pioneers with a vision to effect school change to become leaders in school reform. Albert Shanker believed that teachers and unions had a "responsibility to save a dying institution" (Checkley, 1996, p. 4) by convincing a skeptical public that union work is for the good of public education. This could be accomplished when unions helped teachers to ask pertinent questions, to examine all issues from all possible perspectives, and to see all dimensions of the human spirit from all sides of any given issue (Mungazi, 1995). The possible emergent language of unionism, one that enabled the vocal and public support of teachers for equitable schools in a just democratic society, could be an invaluable support for true school reform.

The dynamic field of education plays a central role in American society and thus can generate substantive public conversation about the goals of democracy and public schooling. Collaborative talk about what is real, true, troubling, and challenging in public education leads to a genuine sense of inquiry. While such inquiry inevitably will reveal problems, such as persistent inequity and unfairness in the present national construction of educational opportunities, it is invaluable to developmental conceptualization of national goals. Educational leaders need not have all the answers, but they need to model ways of continually seeking answers to the best possible questions about the role of public schooling in meeting the needs of all the children of all the people of America.

ACTIVITIES TO ENHANCE UNDERSTANDING

1. *Media policy study*. For the next 6 weeks, cut out all the articles, editorials, or letters to the editor related to educational issues in your local newspaper. At the end of that time period, do the following:
   - Sort the articles into *topics* (e.g., funding, testing, standards) and write a brief summary of the content of each major topic you have identified.
   - Examine each topic to identify *themes* within topics (e.g., within the topic of testing, concern about competition with other nations, competition between schools, abilities of children who experience disadvantage). Write a brief summary of these themes and analyze why you think they have emerged for public discussion.
2. *Teacher and administrator interviews about unions*. Identify at least one public school classroom teacher who belongs to a union, and one public school administrator of a school with a unionized faculty. Interview each in the following areas:

- What are the positive benefits of teacher unionism?
- What are the drawbacks of teacher unionism?
- What are the public perceptions of teacher unionism?
- How might teachers utilize unionism to enhance their leadership in the area of school reform?

Write a brief summary of the interviews and draw conclusions about the current status of teacher unionism in the context of school reform.

7

Educational Language and the Everyday

Education is the life of our national community and the hope of all our children. We thus need a stubborn resolve to examine the health of our schools and search for ways to improve them (Joyce, Wolf, & Calhoun, 1993). School improvement ultimately requires educators to choose one action over another. Whenever educators make choices within schools, they are engaging in moral behavior. *Moral*, in the case of schools, ultimately applies to kinds of valuing, to judgments of good and bad, right and wrong, and to the relationship between those judgments and actions (Greene, 1973). School language, which infuses judgments and actions into the total learning environment, thus provides a great context for meaningful reform.

EVERYDAY TALK IN THE LIFE OF SCHOOLS

This chapter will focus on everyday talk in schools. This is the talk—often private or casual—that builds the language environment and ultimately affects outcomes for children. Educators who accept the premise that *talk is action*, and that *descriptive language about children represents a professional behavior*, will be able to take a critical look at the role of language in their own institutions.

Education Is Communication

Life in schools is characterized by human communication—the language (silent and spoken) that permeates the environment and affects relationships, interactions, efforts, and outcomes. Classroom teachers play a key role in the educative communication of the school, but the language environment also is determined by *every adult who works and interacts with the children*. Principals, specialists, lead teachers, and others who function in positions of modeling or leadership have a tremendous influence on the language environment of the school. Similarly, school secretaries, clerks, custodians, lunchroom aids, parent volunteers, and many others also respond and contribute to the language environment of any institution.

Teachers play a leadership role in efforts to understand and change negative uses of school language. Administrators also set a critical stage of expectations concerning the use of deficit terminology and the tone and content of professional conversations about children and families. Teachers and administrators ultimately have many opportunities to collaborate in the construction of a sensitive and positive language environment, and should hold one another (and all other school volunteers and employees) accountable for following their example.

Language Is Action

This book began with the premise that educational language is an active behavior with important professional ramifications. "Just saying it" is quite different from saying it and knowing that the saying has created consequences of importance. A basic premise of this chapter is that linguistic communications in schools are *speech acts* with full-fledged consequences (Caws, 1996). J. L. Austin, who in 1962 gave a series of semantic lectures at Harvard University, examined this very important question—"Can saying it make it so?" (p. 7). During these lectures, he cited several examples of what he called performative sentences: "I do" (marriage vow), "I name this ship the *Queen Elizabeth*," "I bet you sixpence it will rain tomorrow" (p. 5). His examples, Austin believed, made it clear that to utter a sentence was not to *describe* but "to do it" (p. 6).

Of course, educators are not linguists and scarcely have the time to engage in lengthy academic analyses of the role and function of their language in schools. They can and should, however, *fully recognize the power of words to name potential, ability, intentions, and commitments*—and thus to create virtual reality in the school setting. It is interesting to note Austin's (1962) further belief that the outcomes of performative expressions might be thought of as "happy or unhappy," as exemplified by "I censure" or "I approve" (p. 83). His ideas remain relevant for educators who do indeed either welcome or disinvite, and approve or censure—often in response to student classification or confidential information about students and their families.

Happy linguistic outcomes can occur in schools on a daily basis when students are endowed with a spirit of possibility, when opportunities are created through growth-seeking words, and when expressions of hope seek the healing of damaged lives. On the other hand, unhappy outcomes can be connected with public naming of failure and deficiency, withholding of opportunity because of negative terminology, and expressed hopelessness about the unfortunate conditions of children's lives. A spirit of professional efficacy, once expressed ("I can do it," "I believe it is possible"), can lighten heavy loads with a prevailing sense of possibility. Everything *said* in a school will be linked ultimately to something that either is happening or will be done. That is why educators are accountable for using language to state ethical and positive intentions for children at all times.

Some who read the above section might argue that it is not language itself, but the attitudes and beliefs that underlie language, that must be addressed. "You will never change educational language," some might argue, "until the problematic attitudes that underlie it are addressed." While a continued professional focus on attitude and belief is a key component of change in the use of language, *language must be viewed as an important behavior in and of itself.* Why? Consider the case of a doctor who works with patients affected with terminal illness. No matter how ill each patient might be, there is some slight statistical chance of recovery. Now, the experienced doctor may have a feeling that each of the current patients is going to die. Nonetheless, his saying, "Each of my patients will soon die," is very different from his saying, "Each of my patients has some statistical chance of recovery." Professional and ethical standards cannot dictate what that doctor believes, but they can dictate his choice of words within the institutional setting. No matter the underlying attitude, the doctor's awareness of the fact that his words directly affect the behaviors of all around him toward the patients makes him ethically accountable for creating the context of hope. This is no less true for educators, whose use of language creates a world of positive or negative conditions for their students.

EDUCATIONAL LANGUAGE AND PROFESSIONAL ACCOUNTABILITY

The words of professionals inevitably convey their sense of accountability. Imagine consulting an attorney about a difficult divorce and custody suit, and hearing her say: "I'll take your case, but this kind of legal problem is really beyond the skill of lawyers. The case is too complicated, the law is unclear, and the parents inevitably are creating unnecessary problems." What is missing is the sense of the *compelling commitment* of the professional to seek the best outcome in spite of barriers. While we would expect the attorney to inform us of the reasons why the case is difficult, and the possible outcomes of trial, we also would listen carefully for an indication that the professional has the knowledge to handle the case well and the determined persistence to seek a positive resolution.

Professional accountability is the expression of a collective desire to maintain the highest standard of practice (Henry, 1993). Educators, like all other professionals, should self-designate standards and then make them available for public scrutiny (Holdsworth, 1993). By opening its deeply held beliefs to public scrutiny, a profession can better shape the expectations of others, while it also protects the maintenance of standards throughout its ranks (Parker, 1993). A profession should perceive itself in the same way it expects those in the public to perceive it. Central to professional self-perception must be a powerful commitment to do what is best for the client (Shea, 1997).

Accountability Reflects a Moral Code

Accountability in a profession assumes a moral adherence to established standards that protect clients. Sockett (1993) suggests that a professional code of practice should focus on four areas: (1) accountability (described as moral obligation), (2) trust, (3) congruence with public claims, and (4) a moral stance toward professional accountability. The code is thus the statement of the collective service ideal of the profession (Airaksinen, 1993). If an educational moral code is indeed present in a refocused language of education, it will be very much in evidence in widespread school practice. "Our discourse and our vocabulary in teaching will become very different as we use a moral language in teaching and education" (Sockett, 1993, p. 13).

"All well and good in the ivory tower," an understandably frustrated teacher might say, "but how does simple conversation in the course of a school day attain such lofty moral ideals?" Consider the following examples:

Edward is a second-grade teacher in a district with the policy of full inclusion of all children with special needs. Many teachers do not support the policy, but Edward has made the decision to support it. One of his students this year has frequent epileptic seizures, some severe. Edward has had to work closely with her doctor and parents throughout the year, and in the process has learned a great deal about epilepsy. He has actively helped all the children in the class to understand the seizures and to remain friendly with their affected classmate. When one of Edward's colleagues asks, "Do you really think it is fair to ask you to accommodate a problem that serious in your classroom?" Edward responds, "This situation has helped me to become a better teacher, and has helped my students to develop more sensitivity toward one another. It is difficult for me, but far more difficult for my student to manage her seizures. I am pleased to share her challenge with her, and I really think she is doing well in her studies." (What if Edward had said, "I don't know how they can expect us to deal with impaired kids when we have the needs of our normal students to consider"?)

Dolores has a child named Beth in her third-grade reading class whose single mother recently died of cancer. Sad and withdrawn, Beth is upset over several different foster placements in the past few months. Dolores is very concerned about her poor performance on recent assessments. Asked by a fellow teacher about Beth's progress, she replies, "I am so concerned about her right now. Naturally she is finding it hard to concentrate. It is sad to know I cannot alleviate her home situation, but I have been able to try a few things at school. I gave her a book on bereavement for children, and moved her to her best friend's cooperative reading group." (What if she had said, "Until her home life gets straightened out, there is not much I can do to help her with her reading problems"?)

Pat has a child in her classroom this year who is exhibiting severe behavior challenges. When the child recently had a violent tantrum during a class trip to a museum, Pat was embarrassed when the manager asked her to remove the entire group from the museum until it was under better control. During a subsequent meeting with the guidance counselor, Pat says, "Let me tell you about what happened at the museum, and maybe you can give me suggestions for helping my student to handle trips. I don't want to leave him behind, but I don't know enough about how to handle his problems right now." (What if she had said, "I was warned about him. I refuse to bring him on another trip, and I think he should be moved to an alternative school"?)

All these teachers, who are under stress from special student-related circumstances, have reflected professional accountability in their statements. They focused on a sense of responsibility to be sensitive and to seek better outcomes for their students. Their statements are moral because they are caring, and those who participate in the dialogue are inevitably affected in their own practice by the commitment and positive position of their colleague. These teachers have taken steps to help their students, and their use of language is also an action reflective of accountability and positive intention.

The Authority to Make Assumptions About Others

Teachers and administrators have the authority to make assumptions about children on a daily basis. Such authority undoubtedly is reflected in the daily use of school language (Smith, 1993). The tone and quality, as well as the content, of verbal interchange is affected by what those in authority assume about students. While overly positive assumptions might cause some problems ("All our students should be able to handle advanced work easily"), overly negative assumptions will cause inevitable harm ("None of our students are capable of handling advanced work"). Educators seeking an ethical school language must determine a way to confront assumptions that are unnecessarily negative and thus damaging to the climate and quality of the institution as a whole.

Rist (1973), who exposed biased professional language in his ethnographic study of an urban school, wrote: "Teachers' assumptions manifest themselves within the classroom setting. These assumptions transform themselves into expectations for individual children, with the result that differential treatment is accorded various members of the same class" (p. 242). He elaborated on the harmful assumptions that seemed to justify potentially harmful attitudes or actions toward some children:

> The basic tenets may be summarized as follows: Middle class students can learn, lower class students cannot; white schools are "good," black schools are "bad"; control is necessary, freedom is anarchy; violence works, persuasion does not; teachers can save a few but will lose many; the school tries, the home will not; and finally only the naive would dispute these beliefs, as the wise know. (p. 241)

How many educators could really claim today that they are not aware of the continuing existence of the above assumptions, on at least some levels or in some institutions? It is far easier to overlook this problem than it is to confront it, because in the process of confrontation we also might bring discriminatory professional attitudes to the attention of the public. However, educational language will not change until negative, cruel, discriminatory assumptions are exposed and eradicated.

The Continuing Moral Choice

If the issues of educational language are to be sufficiently addressed, the moral choices inherent in what is said about children (even in the most secret or casual circumstances) must be acknowledged. It is possible to build the daily presence of a responsible and accountable dialogue; it is equally possible to damage children with irresponsible and uncaring statements on a daily basis. Accountable educators who are determined to speak responsibly must recognize the presence of authority and power in their words. Thompson (1991) reminds us that linguistic expressions, which represent the exchange of power, are loaded with unequal weights. Words can and do represent coercion, constraint, condescension, or even contempt.

Integral to professional accountability is full recognition of the ways in which words control, hurt, limit, or help other people. Educators who become active listeners within the environment of their institutions quickly can become aware of the many ways in which the power and authority of language are used. In spite of truly terrible problems of poverty, abuse, violence, drugs, home and family disruption, and many other barriers to full child development, the accountable educator must speak in a way that takes clear moral responsibility for the best possible outcomes. Of course, all teachers have fears, doubts, questions, and problems. Nonetheless, what they say as professionals, in school and society, must reflect an unswerving commitment to their students.

ETHICS AND PROFESSIONAL LANGUAGE

Educators in schools need active and well-established codes of ethics to help them live up to their own stated goals of accountability. Codes of ethics guide educators in the act of service and help them to rise above disruptive or disappointing circumstances to persist in their chosen acts of investment in the growth of others. Professional ethics represent an explicable set of rules, an ideal, a constellation of expressions that justifies and guides our conduct (Noddings, 1995). Such ethics can serve to establish common professional norms that are guided by a moral point of view and also fully articulate the compact between the profession and larger society (Kultgen, 1988). A code of ethics, once established, represents a serious and challenging obligation for professionals.

> Codes of professional practice provide guidelines and requirements which are meant to be followed by all members of the profession. . . . If a common code is to be effective in sustaining shared values and principles within a profession, divergent practices among subscribers to the code can not be tolerated. (Jackson, 1993, p. 116)

Applying Ethical Codes

The relationship of the language environment of the school to an established code of ethics is promising although complex. As stated throughout this book, the ethics of language are never as simple as "say this" or "do not say that." Schoolpeople need flexibility in decision making about students, often based on standardized assessments or confidential information, but they also need thoughtful common guidelines that enhance professionalism and protect students. *The Code of Ethics of the Education Profession*, first published in 1955 and still adopted by the Representative Assembly of the National Education Association, provides some historical insights into the continuing issues of language and accountability. As it was revised in 1964, the code included the following guidelines under Principle I (Commitment to the Student):

> Withhold confidential information about a student or his home unless we deem that its release serves professional purposes, benefits the student, or is required by law.
> Make discreet use of available information about the student.
> Refrain from commenting unprofessionally about a student or his home. (pp. 12–13)

To the above three points, *Opinion 13* of the Committee on Professional Ethics of the National Education Association (1964) was applied in the case of a teacher (Teacher A) who discussed one of his students with another teacher (Teacher B) in a hallway within hearing of a classmate of the student under discussion. "The teacher commented adversely on the student's mental ability and personal integrity, attributing these deficiencies to the pupil's family background" (p. 45). Teacher B, disapproving of the comments, reported the incident to the local association.

The committee decided that the behavior of Teacher A violated the 1952 code, which provided that a teacher will

> Section 2. Recognize the differences among students and seek to meet their individual needs.
> Section 3. Help to increase the student's confidence in his own home and avoid disparaging remarks which might undermine that confidence. (p. 45)

The committee further stated:

> A teacher is entrusted with the obligations of helping children to develop into happy, useful, self-supporting citizens and of furthering cooperative relationships with the home. These obligations can not be fulfilled . . . when a teacher makes disparaging remarks reflecting on a child's abilities or family background. (p. 45)

The final opinion of the committee of the National Education Association (NEA) acknowledged the complexity of information sharing in schools by stating that

> It is improper for an educator to make remarks in public reflecting on a student's abilities and family background. However, an educator has the right and often the

duty to confer in confidence with colleagues or authorized agencies regarding a student's problems in conduct and adjustment. (p. 13)

The ethic of descriptive language in schools, reflected in the NEA code, has continued to be presented in the ongoing discussion of applied ethics in education. Strike and Soltis (1998) preface their book *The Ethics of Teaching* with the Code of Ethics of the Education Profession adopted by the 1975 NEA Representative Assembly. In that more recent publication, the NEA code states that the educator "shall not intentionally expose the student to embarrassment or disparagement" and "shall not disclose information about students obtained in the course of professional service, unless disclosure serves a compelling professional purpose or is required by law" (p. x).

The NEA code continues to stand as an important standard of support for positive and professional language environments in schools. The successful application of that standard, however, inevitably will require the thoughtful practice of committed educators. Within the school setting, ethical language can emerge only when educators use ethical codes as inspiration for continual reflection on the ways in which professional talk reflects best practice and commitment to children.

Striving for Integrity

Every human service professional struggles at times with the discrepancy between the service ideal and the reality of daily life within the service-providing institution. Problems will always arise in the application of ethical guidelines to actual situations. The true respect of professionals for their ethical code is undermined when it includes specific obligations to which they know perfectly well that they cannot conform under existing circumstances (Jackson, 1993). Therefore, any in-school discussion of ethics and professional language should be realistic and sensitive to routine demands placed on teachers. Divergent viewpoints are inevitable, as are different individual applications of shared professional beliefs. Ethical codes should be monitored continually to be sure that they remain credible (Henry, 1993).

A successful refocus of educational language in any school requires collective recognition that language is an important aspect of the moral nature of education. Teachers should have the opportunity to discuss and share multiple perspectives on the ethical dilemmas of school language. This reciprocal dialogue should be viewed as a search for enlightenment on responsible choices and mutual solutions to professional problems (Noddings, 1988). Dialogue between teachers, and about children and families, should be consistently based on what Strike and Soltis (1998) call the principle of equal respect for persons. This principle requires that educators

1. Treat people as ends rather than means, considering the goals and welfare of others as well as their own
2. Treat people as free, responsible, and rational agents, respecting their choices and enabling them to function responsibly
3. Give equal value to all people and their different interests, entitling them to the same basic rights

It is equal respect for all people that provides a structure of moral integrity to conversations about educational language. Teachers may disagree about whether or not labels for children in special education classes should be openly used in schools, for example, but should base their argument appropriately on what is good for *all children*—all of whom are viewed as equals. Therefore the argument, "I think all of the children should become accustomed to the names we have for human differences, because that will help them to integrate acceptance of differences into their adult lives," is very different from the argument, "The special education children are never going to be as good in school as the regular students, and everyone knows it, so there is no reason to hide the facts or avoid appropriate terminology." Educators sensitive to the moral quality of the talk around them can reflect on the environmental biases that may be skewing their own perceptions of their students. The more they reflect upon and refocus their own habits of speech, the greater the integrity with which they can approach the construction of the total language environment of the school.

The search for ethical integrity can be viewed as the means to a coherence of wholeness about everything educators do and believe (Sockett, 1993). It is important for all involved to be open to the possibility that there is a current lack of integrity in their own behavior or that of others.

> We retain our integrity by having different parts of our life in harmony. Sometimes, perhaps often, there are conflicts between such traditions, or we are unfaithful to them, or we are not true to ourselves. We let our commitments and ideals slip away. We lose our altruism. Then we have to face up to the question . . . am I the sort of person who would do this? Each of us has to face the question of who we are. (Sockett, 1993, p. 154)

Educators who are willing to acknowledge a possible lack of integrity and actively seek to avoid it are better able to rely on ethical codes that guide and protect professional behavior.

It is natural for teachers to have a defensive reaction to unfair criticism, which often is expressed in the process of school reform. Defensiveness, however, all too easily can become resistance to change and improvement where it is truly needed. Therefore, a defensive stance is counterproductive to honest reflection on ethical practice. It may be tempting, for example, to think, "I would never do anything to hurt a child," or "I know that a child's background or color does not influence me." A more honest approach, however, is to recognize the *possibility* that one is capable of discriminatory behavior and must be vigilant in guarding against it. Deceit of oneself or others

> can arise through neglect as much as from direct intention to mislead, and it is on deceit that we must focus. Its ramifications are seen in such issues as censorship, the withholding of relevant information, the hiding behind institutional power, unexamined bias, and perhaps most of all, the neglect or lack of concern for what is true. (Sockett, 1993, p. 64)

Deceit is an ongoing danger when rationalization of classification systems, such as tracking, grouping, and labeling of children, is taking place. The ethical dangers of bias and discrimination must be fully acknowledged when serious decisions are made about the value of people and the resources to which they will have access. Teachers might ask themselves, "Would I allow my own child to remain a student in this school if she received this classification and were thus treated in this manner?" or "When most of the children in our low track come from families on public assistance, how can we be sure that bias is not influencing our decisions about them?" or "If my own child were not in the gifted program in this school, could I be confident that he was receiving an equitable education?" In this process of self-reflection, they might be inspired by this historical statement of the Ethics of the Education Profession (National Education Association, 1964):

> We measure success by the progress of each student toward achievement of his maximum potential. We therefore work to stimulate the spirit of inquiry, the acquisition of knowledge, and the thoughtful formulation of worthy goals. (p. 11)

Enacting an Ethic of Care

Educators need to look beneath their words to seek out their true intention. Ethical goals dictate that intentions of educators, expressed in what they say and do, are characterized by *caring* that outcomes for students are good. Every human encounter presents us with the possibility of a caring occasion, and educators who behave ethically must continually strive to preserve or convert a given relation into a caring relation (Noddings, 1995). Caring is in evidence when the language of teachers helps to affirm the value of students and the possibility of their success. This affirmation exists when students are clearly discussed as equals who are respected regardless of differences in experience and ability.

An ethic of care cannot exist without a parallel sense of obligation for fostering development. Obligation is characterized by the words "I must." Noddings (1995) warns that teachers can reject the obligation of "I must" by shifting to "something must be done" or "someone must do something." This shift allows teachers to remove themselves from a sense of personal agency or, alternatively, to feel that there is actually nothing they can do. If a teacher is comfortable with the abandonment of a sense of obligation, that teacher can no longer care. "Caring requires me to respond . . . with an act of commitment: I commit myself either to overt action on behalf of the cared for . . . or I commitment myself to thinking about what I might do" (p. 11). Thinking about what one might do, within the framework of obligation to try to do something, fosters the sense of inquiry that is so central to a refocused educational language.

Caring is a particularly important concept for teachers whose students encounter significant problems in their lives. I believe that the habit of wondering what can be done counters a tendency to feel hopeless about serious situations. Consider the example of Alfredo, who was born in the United States to parents who were illegal aliens. His parents currently have lost access to public assistance and health insurance, and Alfredo is not receiving appropriate care for his asthma and vision problems. Although he works hard in school, Alfredo sometimes seems hungry, tired, and depressed. His grades, in spite of his persistence, are often low. What conversation might we hope to hear between two of his teachers, who are mindful of the ethic of care?

> "I am so concerned about Alfredo, because I know he can do well in school and he lacks so many things that he needs."
>
> "I know what you mean. I am asking several people in the district about possible resources for his asthma and vision, but I am not sure help is available. In the meantime, at the next team meeting I think we should discuss ways to support his school performance as much as we can. I think that strengthening his literacy skills will help him no matter where his family ultimately decides to move."

Alfredo's hypothetical story is, unfortunately, not an unusual one in many American schools. Teachers often must cope with potentially disabling sadness about trouble in the lives of their students. Children for whom they care deeply may lack health services, adequate food, or even a family of their own. There is no doubt that more social and political support for the needs of these children outside the school would alleviate the real suffering or stress of children and their teachers inside the school. There are definite limits to the reasonable efforts of teachers, not only in terms of classroom instruction but in terms of the emotional strength required to be supportive of children in troubling circumstances. *Caring*, however, presents ethical possibilities in even the most difficult of situations. If nothing else for the moment, caring creates avenues of responsible teacher talk about the problems and limits of teachers' best efforts for their students.

Turning to a very different scenario, what might a teacher do who hears a very different conversation about Alfredo?

"Kids like Alfredo are never going to be able to do well; the school cannot possibly counteract their devastating home lives."

"I know. Ten years ago we had only a handful of children born to illegal aliens in this school. Today we have over a hundred. This situation is dragging down our test scores, scaring away good families from our school, and demoralizing our staff."

The ethical teacher can choose to speak on Alfredo's behalf, or remain silent in order to reflect on how best to respond to the dilemmas of such a conversation. Caring about Alfredo, and knowing that he is already hurt by the attitudes of some of the students and staff members, the teacher can wonder, "What must I do to improve this situation?" If a school district has a professional code of ethics related to school language, the ethical educator can refer to it and make an appropriate decision about a responsible way in which to respond to such a negative, hopeless, and inherently harmful conversation. (Chapter 8 of this book will examine the development and possible use of such an ethical code in individual educational institutions.) In any case, however, the educator who is confronted with inappropriate and potentially damaging professional language has the option of playing a role of advocacy in the movement of the school toward a refocused educational language.

CHILD ADVOCACY AND EDUCATIONAL LANGUAGE

A spirit of child advocacy helps educators to transcend their daily responsibilities in order to have a wider influence within their profession and in the greater society. They can better seek to use their own power and beliefs to strengthen the commitment of many others to the needs of children. The continuing goal of advocacy is a caring and protective movement toward optimal growth and development in every child (Fennimore, 1989).

Advocacy, although it inevitably creates tension and conflict, also arouses the passions of educators and thus can help them to overcome discouragement or despair. As educators become comfortable with an assertive stance of advocacy, they have more confidence to express their commitments openly, to take advantage of opportunities to influence policies, and to take personal responsibility for shaping the climate of their schools and communities (Fennimore, 1995).

Educators who view themselves as advocates are better able to accept the conflict inherent in balancing the ideals of their profession with discouraging daily realities. They can develop a stronger sense of personal, professional, and moral agency, which enables them to take responsibility for institutional and social change. Because the gains of advocacy are often difficult to measure, and the work of advocates so often falls short of idealistic goals, advocates need to believe that any persistent effort for the cause of children always contributes to the public good. Win or lose, courageous efforts on behalf of children permeate the social and moral environment, and provide inspiration to others. Advocacy is ultimately a sense of adventure in the uncharted waters of a stronger democracy and a better future for children.

Some educators who are advocates have the skills, endurance, and passions that enable them to deal with the strong conflicts inherent in public controversy. Many other educators who also have a passionate interest in the well-being of students decide that their advocacy efforts are best expressed within their own employment situation. They may take extra steps to help individual children (case advocacy) or groups of children (class advocacy) who are falling behind within the system, or they may take a strong stand on issues of institutional change and improvement. The spirit of advocacy often may motivate them to grow from an impartial stance on controversial issues into the establishment of a strong personal position that is expressed in daily institutional interactions. Each educator who becomes an advocate ultimately finds a way to share the burdens of children and to represent them in ways that motivate social and political change.

The need to refocus educational language within one's school or program provides an excellent opportunity for advocacy. In the context of discussing the ways in which students are spoken about and described, important ethical issues will arise for consideration. Advocates can assert the rights of the students to respect for their human dignity and potential, and create links between a refocused language and a more positive and encouraging school environment.

Advocacy for the Refocus of Educational Language

The refocus of educational language, like any significant change in education, inevitably will involve some conflict. Imagine, for example, some hypothetical negative responses to the suggestion that descriptive language itself is a serious professional issue:

> If it isn't one thing, it's another. Now we are supposed to start thinking about talk within the privacy of our own classrooms or the teachers' lounge. We all need to express ourselves, don't we?

I have been teaching diverse children in different schools for 20 years, and I really don't think that the conversations I've had with other teachers have had one thing to do with my professional effectiveness.

As a school administrator, I deal on a daily basis with budget cuts, threats to teachers, and student violence. Please don't tell me that I am supposed to take time out to be concerned with the way the educators in my building talk to one another.

I really don't see the connection between what educators say to one another and outcomes for students. I mean, does saying something really change anything?

Advocates for the refocus of educational language may well encounter such reactions and will need to respond to them with thoughtful responses. The best approach may well be transcendence over basic issues of educational linguistics into a deeper social analysis of the ways in which life in institutions is affected by the quality of communal language. Talk can be inspirational and energizing ("I am determined to do the best I can") or demoralizing ("I feel as though I am completely powerless"). Advocates for the refocus of educational language can argue that the infusion of moral and democratic issues into school talk can revitalize a communal sense of mission.

Any viable form of schooling needs to be informed by a passion and faith in the necessity of struggling in the interest of creating a better world. These seem like strange words in a society that has elevated the notion of self-interest into the status of a universal law. And yet our very survival depends on the degree to which the principles of communality, human struggle, and social justice aimed at improving the privileges of all groups eventually prevail. (Giroux, 1984, p. 39)

Also, advocates can argue that the integrity of any educational institution should be reflected in the presence of a language characterized by commitment to and passion for social justice. Members of institutions have the responsibility to invest them with their own ideals and values, and the energy necessary to fight for what they believe in (Sockett, 1993).

Advocacy for a Language of Responsible Community

Advocates often are assumed to be people who are fighting for rights—their own or those of others. When the language of advocacy is overly focused on the concept of rights, however, an important dialogue about social responsibility can be lost. Glendon (1991), in her thoughtful analysis of rights talk, expresses concern that the ever-emergent portfolio of individual and group rights makes it "hard to give voice to common sense or moral intuitions and gets in the way of rational political discourse" (p. 14). Glendon argues that the replacement of a search for understanding of the ecology of human personhood and social policy with talk of rights "contributes to the erosion of the habits, practices, and attitudes of respect for others that are the ultimate and surest guarantees of human rights" (p. 137).

A dialogue of rights often can be necessary, but it should be placed within the larger context of community responsibility. Advocates for refocused language can seek enhancement of the spirit of group responsibility. For example, if a colleague were to say, "I am really tired of parents coming in here to protect the rights of their children, without caring one bit about the rights of teachers," it might be tempting to respond that "the children do have rights, and the parents have every right to protect them." A more productive response could be, "I wonder how we could have some conversations between parents and teachers to talk about the ways in which we can solve some of the problems that are upsetting these parents. It would be good to establish a framework of mutual responsibility as a path to equal rights." Advocates should make connections continually between rights and the responsibility of all members of a community to create security and respect for all other members.

No one in a responsible community has the right to harm another with prejudiced talk or action. In contrast, everyone in a community has the right to be safe from prejudice. All within the community thus must be particularly aware of the need to confront discrimination and bias when and where they occur. Prejudice poses serious dangers to all in society, not only because of the harm to its victims but also because of the damaging effects of hatred and rage on the general society. It is therefore a moral problem that requires a strong and assertive response.

Zero Tolerance for Prejudiced Talk

Advocates for social causes, whether alcohol-related car accidents, environmental hazards, advertisements for teen-age smoking, or a variety of others, know that many people must get involved if serious human problems are going to be solved. Involvement often means taking a personal stand, rather than looking the other way, when those around us are engaging in wrongful or dangerous actions. Position taking is difficult for many people, no matter how strong their beliefs, because it somehow feels as though they are being impolite or intrusive. However, responsible community members must take a position on issues that are central to human safety and dignity (Fennimore, 1994).

Some analysts of social policy have suggested that the concept of *zero tolerance*, or a general agreement within a group to implement an absolute refusal to condone or ignore a violation of ethics or law, can strengthen the willingness of individuals to confront wrongful actions of others. An example might be a high school, formerly plagued with drug problems, in which all parents and faculty agree to confront and report all drug use to administrators and other authorities. Advocates for a refocused educational language might wonder if the concept of zero tolerance might be applied to the problem of blatantly prejudiced talk about children in schools.

A stance of zero tolerance in the area of prejudiced statements would mean that caring professionals would not ignore egregious violations of language ethics involving discriminatory, racist, or clearly biased statements. These would include openly derogatory judgments of ethnic groups, racial jokes or slurs, blanket assumption of inferior intelligence or ability in any ethnic group, or any other obvious insult to the appearance, behavior, language, or culture of any group. In such instances, educators would agree to make a strong and clear personal belief statement such as the following:

> That joke makes me very uncomfortable, because I think that prejudiced beliefs about (that group) ultimately creates harm to them in our society.

> I do not agree that children from (that group) are less intelligent, and I want to do everything in my power as a professional to help them develop their high potential.

> I do not believe that such an expression is appropriate for use in our school. It is insulting to our students and can create a painful and rejecting climate.

Such responses may not extinguish the prejudiced beliefs of the speaker, but they will assert a humane and protective stance toward the students into the language environment of the school. Some discomfort inevitably will exist between the two speakers, but failure to clarify the hearer's personal position would leave the prejudiced speaker with the unfortunate impression that the hearer agreed with what was said.

Sergiovanni (1992) suggests that moral outrage is an appropriate response whenever good purposes toward children are being thwarted; educators always have the right to be outraged at the abuse and disempowerment of others. In fact, Sergiovanni believes that moral outrage can be an acceptable form of leadership that, when successful, encourages every member of the school community to "display outrage when the standard falls" (p. 132). There may be many grey areas in the judgment of the language of others, but there should be no equivocation in the moral response to blatantly prejudiced comments made in educational institutions.

The Process of Refocusing Language

While educators should take an unswerving stance on the egregious prejudiced comment, I think that they also must give more flexible consideration to the many situations in which the true meaning of what is said is far less clear. The intentionality of language use in human beings is very complex and is shaped by diverse cultural, personal, and institutional understandings. Many educators today have been immersed in deficit terminology for their entire careers and have developed ingrained habits of language use. Also, the climates of many schools have long supported the disposition to use negative descriptive language about students, particularly when the schools serve highly challenged child populations. Therefore, the habitual language about "low groups" or "single-parent families" or "dysfunctional communities" or "at-risk kids" or "free lunch children" is actually (though unfortunately) part of what has been accepted institutional practice. For all these reasons, a rigid application of zero tolerance as an initial policy approach to the *total* reform of school language is likely to be counterproductive.

A true refocus of language, while highly desirable, instead will require a long and thoughtful process of growing self- and group awareness. It is important that such a process not be damaged by overly confrontational behaviors in situations of questionable meaning or intent. All educators should understand the ease with which words can be misunderstood or misinterpreted; all educators should know that the process of learning requires understanding and support from peers. As dialogue in supportive educational communities continues to examine the uses and abuses of educational language, more and more educators will begin to *hear* themselves and recognize habits and dispositions of speech that might be improved. Eventually, the development of ethical codes concerning school language (discussed in Chapter 8) will place greater pressure for change on those who continue to use disparaging words to describe their students.

The words of each member of a school community have a resounding impact on the quality of the language environment. Educators who embark on an analysis of the use of language in their schools, and resolve to create a responsible and positive language environment, thus can make great strides in improving the quality of daily interchange and in creating a more protective educational environment for children.

ACTIVITIES TO ENHANCE UNDERSTANDING

1. *Responding to prejudiced comments.* Participate in a discussion of the social dilemmas involved in confronting prejudice in others. How can we respond

when beloved family members hold deeply prejudiced beliefs, or when long-time friends tell racist jokes? What about the fear of retaliation if we confront people we do not know well about prejudiced comments?

Then discuss the difference between the social and the professional environment. How can educators develop a professional character that allows them to be collegial and yet to feel comfortable with a strong stance on prejudice? Make a plan for developing a relationship with colleagues that allows for strong position taking when the need arises (e.g., how do you build and maintain professional distance in the social environment of the school?).

2. *Infusing advocacy and moral stance into language.* Select a topic in teacher education that tends to be controversial (i.e., preparation for status quo vs. preparation to be a change agent in schools). Engage in a small-group discussion in which each member contributes ideas that reflect strong statements of personal belief ("If new teachers are outspoken they are going to get fired") and personal commitment ("I am committed to support the concept of inclusion in any school in which I eventually teach"). Then discuss the personal feelings and responses engendered by strong statements. How did this discussion differ from some of the less personal discussions that often take place in staff meetings or college classrooms? How might educators start to feel more comfortable with a language centered on advocacy and moral concerns?

8

Developing a Code
of Ethics Concerning
Educational Language

Every profession has the ethical duty to society (including the internal societies of its own institutions) to widen the understanding, appreciation, and utilization of the ethics it most values (Parker, 1993). Since the use of language is the most visible daily expression of values in a school, it deserves close ethical attention. Administrators and classroom teachers alike can make a decision to take a focused ethical look at the language environment of their school. Although the idea might seem novel at first, it soon will become apparent that the study of the school language environment opens the door to discussion of many important issues of educational quality and school climate. Ultimately, a critical analysis of school language is likely to bring fundamental democratic ideas and questions about equality and excellence to the surface.

CREATING A SCHOOL CODE OF LANGUAGE ETHICS

The ultimate goal of a school examination of the language environment should be the collaborative creation of a code of ethics concerning educational language. (See the discussion of ethical codes in Chapter 7.) If a school already has a code of ethics in place, a section on language might be added. Or, the entire code might be rewritten to include responsiveness to issues of language environment. The process of developing the code, important in and of itself, should involve all members of the school community in critical reflection on the role of language in education. The product, the written ethical code, will be effective only if it reflects a process of thoughtful participation on the part of those who ultimately will seek to live by it.

Because each school will have very different circumstances to consider, individualized planning to refocus the language environment will be important. One school, for example, might have no formal tracking of students and a stated commitment to the full inclusion of children who have special needs without the use of identifying labels. Another school may have systematic tracking, clearly identified special education classes, and ability grouping within all regular classes. Again, one school may serve a fairly homogeneous and advantaged population, while another serves students who represent wide socio-economic and ethnic diversity. Many teachers in one school may share the cultural and ethnic identity of the students; many teachers in another school may not. All these individual school characteristics will require differential examination of language issues under the shared umbrella of commitment to democratic principles in society.

The Integrity of an Ethical Code

Any ethical code must have integrity in order to be effective. Unfortunately, it may appear that many teachers or administrators have jaded views toward the expenditure of time on the creation of ethical codes. In some cases, this may be because the people involved are feeling overwhelmed or undersupported in terms of immediate professional concerns. If such is the case, the importance of a code of ethics might be discussed in the context of improving the overall emotional and professional climate. A refocused language climate might open the door to many new ways of supporting and encouraging all within the school.

In other cases, reluctance might be attributed to past negative experiences of some individuals who made a voluntary contribution of time to develop other written policies or codes that were never implemented. They might say or feel that "it is just a waste of time" to sit and talk about ideas when so many efforts never really seem to get off the ground. In such cases it might be helpful to establish the intrinsic value of dialogue, and the ways in which dialogue about school language can strengthen commitments to solve many real and pressing problems. Those who advocate for an ethical code also might counter resistance and build integrity by establishing specific ways in which a refocused language might be a dynamic and observable force within the school.

Areas of Emphasis for Language Codes

It is helpful at the outset to identify and organize both general and specific areas of the school language environment that will be considered in the process of creating a code. The suggested *general* areas for focus are (1) the overall tone of institutional language and the expressed attitude toward students, and (2) professional decisions about what should (and should not) be said about students within the school setting. The suggested *specific* areas (introduced in Chapter 1) are (1) indiscriminate use of deficit terminology, (2) classification and tracking of students, and (3) confidentiality of personal information about students. Teachers and administrators probably will find it best to begin with the general areas and then move into the specific areas as the code develops. My discussion in this chapter will seek to provide guidance to educators who decide to develop a school code of language ethics. It will follow the order established above and will utilize the efforts of the hypothetical Woodwell school as an example.

EXAMINING THE GENERAL LANGUAGE ENVIRONMENT OF A SCHOOL

Chapter 1 of this book discussed scenarios in which visitors to schools developed very different impressions based on exposure to the overall tone of school language. In doing a self-study that leads to the development of a code of ethics, educators in a school need to think of themselves as visitors and observers. This is a good opportunity to notice the flow of words, conversations, and exchanges of information. How might the language environment be characterized? Is it one that makes it more possible for students and educators alike to do their best work?

What Is the Overall Tone of School Language?

This section is written on the assumption that the educators writing the code are teaching children whose backgrounds are very different from their own. When first considering the general tone of the school language environment, begin with this question: "If I entered my own child's school, what feeling would I like to get about the ways in which the professionals were talking about children?" Any parent would appreciate a school language environment that radiates respect for children and a genuine enthusiasm for their education. An important dimension of such respect and enthusiasm would be faculty expression of the confident assumption that the students have a promising future. Teachers and administrators know very well that they would be reluctant to send their own children to schools where the language environment was depressed and disrespectful, or reflected a lack of faith in the present and future potential of students. The realization that the language environment in the school in which they work would be unsuitable for their own children would provide an excellent start for the development of an ethical code. Here is one of the first discussions that might emerge:

> Our own children do not go to school hungry, or exhausted, or badly frightened by violence. We encourage our own children to obey their teachers and to study hard. How can we expect the same language of hope and respect in their schools and in one that serves a needy and difficult population of children?

The collaborative formulation of answers to questions like the one above will serve as a critical key to the integrity of any ethical code created for the school. Here is a possible answer to the above question:

> The language environment of any school should be far more reflective of the ethics of the profession than of the advantaged or disadvantaged nature of student life. Professional talk in every school can and should reflect respect, kindness, caring, and hope. Nowhere is this more important than in the schools that serve our neediest American children. To allow a school language reflecting harsh and belittling attitudes to interfere with the intellectual progress and emotional health of any of our students would be unconscionable and unacceptable to the ethical beliefs of our profession.

There is no doubt that educators who work with more seriously challenged students do face a more difficult call in the development of ethical use of school language. It is harder to hope when children seem overwhelmed by troubles, and it is harder to respect children if teachers do not feel respected by parents or communities. However, those courageous educators who rise to the challenge of refocusing their school language in the face of adversity can provide all schools and teachers with excellent role modeling.

After all, every school serves some children who are far more challenged than others. While they may not be experiencing the extremes of poverty and violence, even schools that serve a preponderance of advantaged and high-achieving students have their share of difficulties with some children and families. Every school has some issues of hierarchy or stratification, whether overt or covert, that may result in a biased language environment. Equal treatment and equal regard for all students is undoubtedly a challenge to some degree in each and every school in America.

Does the Tone Build Connection and Expectation? Moving now to a more detailed consideration of the tone of school language, it is important to take a close look at expressions of connection to and expectation for students.

Is the tone one of pride ("We have some of the finest students in the city") or disparagement ("Our population falls far below other schools"). Or, if the school is more diverse, could the tone be, "We serve some of the best and worst students in the city"? Does the tone seem to imply that the faculty has high hopes for future student achievement, little expectation of anything beyond the norm, or a routine expectation of low achievement and failure?

Looking beneath the surface, what presumed characteristics of students are reflected in the general language tone? What, for example, does "best" or "worst" really mean to the school faculty? Has the meaning subsumed inappropriate assumptions about socioeconomic, family, racial, or cultural characteristics? Does it rest on information from standardized test scores? Does the meaning create unfair generalizations about the total school population? Does it rest on assumptions created by the school tracking system, or by a magnet or other elite program with special admission requirements? These questions and others will require teachers and administrators to think very carefully about how they generally describe their students and why they describe them as they do.

If the overall tone seems to set the children apart from the faculty, and to place them in a deficit-based context of thought, it is almost certainly interfering with good relationships with the students. Would the faculty allow their own children to attend a school with a similar tone? As Grumet (1988) writes: "Few of us would excuse our own children from their future with the grace and understanding we extend to other people's children. Other people's children are abstract" (p. 173).

Why might the future of some children appear so much more abstract or diminished than that of others in the eyes of teachers and administrators? One answer may be that teachers whose students seem much like their own children (or the way they imagine their own children would be) find it far easier to relate to them. It is natural, after all, to feel a sense of closer association with people whose lives mirror our own. Children can seem more distant to their educators when the economic circumstances of a child's family (current dependence on public assistance or even homelessness), family problems that appear distasteful (addiction or incarceration of a parent), or characteristics of a child (lack of hygiene or adequate dental care) clash with their own social or cultural values.

The problem of abstraction, a form of educational disassociation, can be addressed successfully and solved persistently by a committed school faculty. First, *all educational professionals* should reinforce language ethics that value and embrace all students regardless of circumstances. This means that educators in more advantaged schools must take care, in their own use of language, not to disassociate themselves and their students from the "kinds of children" in other schools. If all educators adopt ethics that protect all children from harmful and deficit-laden assumptions, teachers in schools that serve less-advantaged children will not feel so isolated and discouraged.

Educational language in any school that avoids bias and remains open to human possibilities forms a stronger professional community. Children within such a community can be better accepted as individuals, and their teachers can better appreciate their real strengths and challenges. It is important to remember that children in all schools, including the most advantaged, may be disabled, distressed, or delayed for a wide variety of reasons. Also, children in schools ranging from the least to the most advantaged may have caring parents, warm extended families, strong church associations, and many other wonderful resources. If the language tone of *any* school seems to imply that every child in the school is the *same*, there is an unquestionable need for reflection and refocus.

Is the Tone Focused on School and Learning? Educational language within a school should be focused most heavily on the primary goal of supporting successful learning and optimal personal development of students. If the tone instead is centered around perception and discussion of the personal lives and characteristics of students (particularly if these are viewed as deficient), the language environment is almost certainly flawed. How should students be discussed, and what about them should be discussed? To answer these questions, the school faculty should move from a discussion of the overall tone of educational language to a closer examination of its actual content. Educational language serves a special professional purpose, and thus should be far more structured and focused than language outside of the school.

What Should Be Said and Not Be Said in School?

It is not possible to create a recipe for ethical discussion of personal information and professional observations about children. Teachers and administrators often need to be trusted as the best judges of what they really need to share and know about children in order to serve them well. To deserve that trust, however, educators must acknowledge their full responsibility to protect vulnerable children from inappropriate or unnecessary predictions and from dissemination of potentially damaging data.

Adults can, after all, protect their own privacy and avoid disclosure of sensitive personal information that could lead to damaging judgments on the part of others. Children in schools, unfortunately, have no control over exposure of sensitive and potentially damaging information. They depend without choice on the professionals with access to confidential information about them, who hopefully will honor the responsibility to protect their privacy and to avoid unsound judgments, observations, or predictions. Failure to honor that responsibility can result in statements like these:

> His brother was a dropout, and I think he is very likely to follow the same pattern.

> Judging from her performance last year, I doubt very much that she can finish this year on grade level.

> When I saw those two brothers fighting on the playground, I just knew that their parents must be using drugs again.

Educators who are constructing a code of ethics concerning the language environment will benefit from discussion about the special qualities of *professional* talk (as compared with talk with friends or family members outside the school). During such a discussion, comparison with the profession of psychotherapy might be illuminating. Although a therapist appears to be *talking* with a client, the use of language is carefully geared to the specific needs of the client and the delineated role of the therapist. Ethics dictate that conversations among therapists who share a practice, while collegial and congenial, never would routinely involve sharing of personal information about clients. Professional collaboration among several therapists, if it were necessary to best serve the client, would be done in private and with the client's permission.

Although teachers are not therapists, they should be aware of links between their work and that of other professionals who serve clients (students in this case) through the use of language and who gain access to deeply personal information in the process. Educators very much need to create a strong delineation between professional and casual uses of language in schools. The use of language, first of all, should be geared specifically to the needs of the student. School language is suitable when it informs, guides, explains, and shares understanding—as long as it serves and protects the growth and well-being of the students. Likewise, language among professionals in the school is suitable as long as it supports collaboration and understanding, and embodies restraint in terms of saying things or sharing information that will harm students.

While a more detailed discussion of confidentiality is included later in this chapter, it should be noted here that educators frequently must differentiate between information that should and should not be shared in the context of the schools. It may be helpful to reflect on two general methods of differentiation in the area of school language: (1) information that *must* be shared, as opposed to information that does not require full elaboration, and (2) comments that ethically might be made in a casual social atmosphere but that are inappropriate within the professional context of the school.

The consideration of information that should and should not be shared can be illuminated by the following example of a child who is transferring from one classroom to another in the same school. Her new teacher probably should know that she becomes easily upset and is tearful throughout the day because of a recent move to a foster home due to family problems. He probably does not need to know (if her present teacher somehow became aware of it) that her father has an arrest and addiction record, and has had multiple troubled marriages. If this young girl had violent tantrums right after her placement, but has shown consistent emotional development in the past 6 months, her second teacher may not need to know about the earlier problems. Discussing them might damage his expectations toward a child who actually is making great progress in dealing with a very difficult personal problem.

The problem of casual social comments that are not appropriate in a professional setting can be examined through a discussion of conversation in the teachers' lounge. While teachers ethically might share casual conversation about their own personal lives, family events, and social activities while resting in this room, they should maintain strict adherence to the ethics code concerning language about students. Any confidential information gained in the performance of professional responsibilities should be protected in the total school environment. Even the most private conversations may harm the dispositions of others toward students and may unfairly influence student teachers and other visiting professionals in the school.

Many teachers will find that sharing feelings (not confidential professional information) with loved ones or good friends outside the school will help them deal with routine problems. If faculty stress or frustration seems uncomfortably high, the administration might seek to provide the opportunity for protected discussion of professional problems mediated by sympathetic and well-trained facilitators. Individual teachers also might decide to take advantage of counseling services provided through their unions or school districts to help them with periods of stress and personal or professional difficulty.

The refocus of school language will require a great deal of reflection, sensitivity, and insight. Many long-term habits and assumptions on the part of faculty will need to be questioned, and every educator in the school will need to be willing to participate in construction of a more positive and professional language.

Example of a School Examining a General Language Environment

The teachers and administrators of Woodwell Elementary School, located in a mid-sized city, have decided to undertake a self-study of the school language environment. The city school board, some time earlier, had decided to hire independent evaluators to assess the climate of all city schools. The faculty of Woodwell had been quite surprised to see in the report that their school was "characterized by pervasive negative expectations for a large number of children." Although first upset and defensive about the report, many of the teachers did recall that their conversations with the evaluators had focused mainly on the problems of the students.

Indeed, the report referred to some of their statements about single-parent families, public assistance, addiction problems, poor student motivation, low test scores, and violence in the community. On reflection, the faculty realized that they had stressed these problems so the evaluators would understand the difficulty and complexity of their jobs. However, they now realized, they inadvertently had created the impression that their own attitudes and actions were unnecessarily negative.

The Woodwell faculty believed that they were far more positive and enthusiastic than had been portrayed and were concerned that they had created such a strong impression of low expectations. It thus seemed important to evaluate ways in which children were described and spoken about during the school day. The teachers decided to spend a month engaged in active listening to formal and informal language within the school. A committee of teachers and administrators developed and distributed a list of questions to assist the entire faculty in informal observation and reflection:

1. If I were a parent of children in this school, how might I respond to the conversations that take place in classrooms, hallways, the teachers' lounge, and faculty meetings?
2. If I were experiencing some of the economic dilemmas of the families in our school, how might I respond to the ways in which public assistance or single-parent families were discussed in the school environment?
3. Does it sometimes seem that negative information is being shared about children when it is not necessary to do so?
4. Do I hear positive conversations about children that indicate high regard for their ability without unnecessary mention of their family, community, or socioeconomic circumstances?
5. Do I hear our students addressed in classrooms and hallways in a manner that is consistently characterized by respect for their personal value and well-being?
6. Do I hear efforts made to describe the strengths and interests of children in the school who are known to have serious problems or disabilities?
7. Do I ever hear statements that reflect blatant prejudice, humor disparaging any ethnic group, assumptions of intellectual or moral inferiority in any ethnic group, or any other bias?

8. Do I overhear conversations in the teachers' lounge that might violate ethics of confidentiality or might appear to be overly negative about students and their families?

Along with the above questions, the staff were asked to evaluate the following draft of a first paragraph of the proposed school code on language ethics:

> As dedicated educators in the Woodwell School, we acknowledge the existence of problems in the lives of students and families and barriers in both social institutions and social environments to the optimal development of many of our students. Yet, we seek to implement a school language characterized by expectation of student success and expectation of our own professional efficacy. We also seek a school language that differs from ordinary social language outside our professional environment because it is consistently geared toward support of the well-being and academic attainment of children. We strongly discourage any professional language that denigrates either the present abilities or future potential of students or teachers. In addition, we choose to take a firm stand against any statements or implications of prejudice or bias in the language of any professional, staff member, visitor, or volunteer in our school. Finally, we consider the teachers' lounge to be a place of rest and refreshment but seek there to also hold to our ethics of confidentiality and professionalism. When colleagues express stress and frustration, we support their engagement of district support services to help them through difficult experiences. Our aim always is a language environment that provides the strongest possible foundation for excellence in education and equity in the provision of access to the best offerings of this school for all students.

SPECIFIC AREAS OF LANGUAGE ENVIRONMENT IN A SCHOOL

After a faculty has had the opportunity to discuss the overall language environment, it will be better prepared to begin to address more specific and complex questions. Which labels are appropriate, and which are derogatory and unnecessary? When does labeling lead to informed practice, and when does it create bias? How should tracks or groups be discussed within the school? How should ability be discussed, and why? Should standardized test scores be a routine component of school language? Should children who have special needs be openly identified within the school? What confidential information about children and families should teachers know? What should be done when schoolpeople become aware of confidential information about students during casual conversations outside of the school building? How much information should be shared in the normal process of the school day?

Answers to these and many other emergent questions will not be easily identified, and indeed a productive tension may arise in the process of faculty discussion. If the protection and support of the student is the guiding light, however, the ongoing dialogue will provide critical insights into the most productive ways possible to design and implement the language code of ethics. It probably will be most helpful for the school faculty to work progressively through each of the three focus areas: (1) use of deficit terminology, (2) language about classification and tracking, and (3) confidentiality in the school.

The Problem of Deficit Terminology

Deficit terminology, previously discussed in Chapter 5, poses a constant threat to the positive treatment and full development of many students. Once labeled in a negative way, a child faces the loss of respect and resultant barriers to optimal development.

> Respect for persons is the central principle of professional practice. . . . If respect for persons is not both the focus and guiding principle to both professional codes and organization goals, then it follows that the individual will be disadvantaged . . . when individuals are not treated as persons or valued as individuals, unethical practices occur. (Henry, 1993, p. 146)

The threat of deficit terminology to children should no more be tolerated than health and safety hazards within a school. Every ethical code on school language should reflect a strong decision on the ways to control the potential harm of this form of language to children.

Educators sometimes feel as though they are pressured to label children in order to receive resources for them. Many state and federal programs that provide funding to schools do require some form of labeling and classification of children. However, this labeling does not have to be incorporated into regular talk within schools. Labels of any kind should not be incorporated into routine conversation ("I had a whole group of SED kids in my class last year") and should not be used at all unless they serve a clear and positive purpose (perhaps during a meeting in which teachers are sharing ideas for inclusion of children with physical disabilities in their classrooms).

Any term that implies deficit or dysfunction is potentially harmful, so its use must be restricted in the best interest of the child. Even when the terms are necessary to receive funding or services for the child, one rule should always apply: "If this were my own child, would I want this label openly and routinely applied to her or him in daily school conversations?" If the answer is "no," then responsible educators should restrict the use of the term whenever possible. There are other more global terms, such as "at risk," "low income," or "dysfunctional family," that carry unnecessary implications of deficit. Educators should be on guard against such poorly defined and negative terminology because it leads to bias and unfounded assumptions. Also, deficit terms should not be used when they are not fully understood in terms of etiology, and when they do not lead to funding or special services.

For example, educators in one school might learn through medical records that some children were exposed to crack cocaine in utero. However, there are no special services for those children in the school, and there is little or no knowledge about the ways in which the children were and were not affected. It therefore would be unethical to call the children "crack babies" or to refer to their exposure to drugs in utero in any routine way, because there is little understanding of their condition and no provision of intervention services. The deficit terminology thus could serve only to lower expectations or create bias.

Example of a School Examining Use of Deficit Terminology

The teachers and administrators of the Woodwell School have turned their attention to the specific issues of deficit terminology in the school language environment. A consultant-led staff workshop helped them to identify the terms routinely used in the school and then to separate the terms into categories. One category was *necessary terms that must be incorporated into the ethical code*, and the other category was *terms that should be eliminated from school use*.

The faculty decided that the following terms would be retained, but that their use would be altered to fit the new code of language ethics:

Learning disabled
Title I
Special Needs I (Behavior)
Special Needs II (Physical)
Gifted and Talented

The terms were retained because they reflected district and school funding and organization. However, the faculty recognized past problems in the assignment of higher (gifted and talented) or lower (special needs) value to students. It was decided that the new code of ethics would suggest limited use of labels in curriculum planning and strict avoidance of routine reference to these classifications in daily school conversation. Many teachers and the school principal expressed hope that, in the development of language that focused on inquiry into student potential, the school would move steadily away from unnecessary and potentially harmful stratification.

The following terms would be avoided because their function was unclear and unrelated to intervention, and because they tended to create biased assumptions:

At risk
Single-parent family
Disadvantaged children
Free and reduced lunch children
Poor community

In the course of discussion, the faculty recognized that the problem of deficit terminology was complicated by the tendency to apply higher-status terms to some children, which also would now be avoided:

Smart kids
Upper middle class
College bound
Parents who care

While complimentary to the children thus designated, the terms had the potential to create bias and to upset the balance of fair and equitable access for all children in the school. The goal of the new ethical code was to support a language environment built on recognition of the developing potential and achievement of all children, without unnecessary designation of high and low status to assumptions about present or future ability.

In addition to identifying the key areas of deficit language, teachers and administrators were asked to evaluate this draft of the related school code on language ethics:

As educators, we acknowledge potential harm of deficit terminology applied to children. We thus seek a school language characterized by terms and descriptions that respect our students as capable individuals. While we recognize that some students are currently achieving on a higher level than others, and that some are more advantaged than others, we seek to avoid complimentary or uncomplimentary terms that serve to stratify our student population. In particular, we seek to eliminate all terminology with the potential to lower expectations for our students from our school language whenever possible. In cases where terminology that applies to specific disorders/disabilities/gifts/program designations currently must continue to be used, we seek to limit its use to areas of absolute necessity and to apply the ethics of confidentiality at all times. Finally, we seek to avoid any global terminology leading to generalizations, and to avoid use of any labeling not directly tied to positive intervention.

Classification and Tracking of Students

It is very important for teachers and administrators who are collaborating on a code of language ethics to confront the challenging area of classifying and tracking students. While several different aspects of that challenge have been explored earlier in this book, what remains to be done is to examine how schools might develop ethical standards in their approaches to classification of students within the language environment. Initial faculty discussion might be based on the interesting fact that ethical considerations historically have blocked educational researchers in the area of teacher expectation from falsely designating groups of students as "dumb" for experimental purposes (Postman, 1966). This has been so *because such negative designation presumably would harm teacher expectations and thus have a negative impact on student achievement and self-perception during the research process.* It is puzzling indeed to wonder why ethics exist to protect children from artificial designations during the process of research, because their harmful nature is recognized, while so many children continue to be labeled in potentially harmful ways during the routine process of schooling.

While the use of testing data to plan appropriate curriculum can be ethically sound, references to groups or tracks should take place only when they serve an important educational purpose. Educators, trusted to make good decisions about disclosure of student abilities, must avoid any casual conversations about classification ("He is one of our ADHD children") or discussion that serves only to lower expectations ("If you are going to student teach in my classroom, you should know up front that I have the lowest children in the school").

Language in schools should reflect acknowledgment that errors can be made in the testing and classification of students, and that tests themselves can be biased. Even when a strong rationale appears for classification (clearly designated disabilities, well-established patterns of need for special intervention, strong indication of unusual ability), questions about appropriate placement and best practice should still exist. Discussion about possible errors in classification can lead to faculty acknowledgment that the permanency of many labels (gifted, disabled) might interfere with accurate observation and assessment of current growth.

Finally, it should be acknowledged that classifications may be created more to serve political than educational purposes, and thus may create artificial or biased assumptions. A certain school district, for example, may test for admission to the limited-access gifted program only during kindergarten. The administrative decision to do this may rest on a desire to compete with private schools to retain high-achieving first graders, and to concentrate the small amount of district funds for gifted education on a population of manageable size. By the time kindergarten class reaches fourth grade, however, it is usually clear that some children who have been designated as gifted are experiencing educational difficulties, while some unidentified children in regular classrooms are now exhibiting exceptional talents or achievements. Although aware of this problem, the district superintendent is unwilling to take on the controversial political task of altering a successful program that attracts many advantaged professional families to the district. This problem creates an invalid classification system and skews the perceptions of children, parents, and teachers.

One of the most serious problems to examine within the area of labeling and classification is the tendency of educators and the public alike to openly assign higher social status to children with positive school designations. Given free reign in schools, this tendency may lead to open valuing of some students over others. ("You are so lucky to have the Bright Horizons class this year. It's bad enough that I had the regular second grade last year; now I have the Title I kids!") To counteract such problems, the school faculty needs to examine why some children are valued more than others, and what can be done to extend stronger acceptance to all children.

Are children valued differently because some are far more difficult to work with than others, or because teachers feel less valued when they are assigned to classes with lower status in the school? If an affirmative answer to either or both questions exists, then part of a successful reform of educational language probably will need to be a parallel restructuring of the current grouping and classification practices within the school. Whether grouping and tracking exist in a given school or not, the process of language reform should help educators find new and better words to discuss children. These words should reflect inquiry, possibility, and acknowledgment that human ability often can transcend the limiting nature of socially constructed categories. They also should create a greater certainty that spoken or unspoken stratifications will not interfere with the creation of a strong school community that is focused on equal treatment of children.

EXAMPLE OF A SCHOOL EXAMINING STUDENT CLASSIFICATION

The teachers and administrators of the Woodwell School are now considering the ways in which tracking and grouping affect the language environment of their school. There are three or four classes on each grade level, and children are placed in classes based on their standardized reading scores the previous year. There is also a transitional kindergarten/first grade for children who appear to be delayed in language or social skills in kindergarten. In addition, some children are identified as learning disabled, special needs (physical or behavioral), or gifted and talented (a magnet program with admission through scores on intelligence tests).

The method of classification and grouping in this school follows district policy. Although the assistant principal and some of the teachers would prefer heterogeneous grouping, that decision would have to be approved district-wide by the superintendent and school board. After consideration of the issues, the school staff has agreed to eliminate references to group levels as a way of identifying classes or children. It was decided that all classes would be identified by room number, teacher, or period ("Please call room 203 to the gym," "I am the parent volunteer assigned to Mr. Smythe's class," "Please give this message to your fourth-period class").

In addition, the teachers have agreed to concentrate on attempts to discuss student behavior and potential in terms of inquiry rather than with a sense of permanence. As a start, whenever it is necessary to identify the current achievement level of any child, the faculty has agreed to try to add a question to their statement ("I was disappointed to see that Sarah's score on reading was very low again this year, because I had been hoping she could move to the next level. I wonder what advice I could give next year's teacher to be sure she has the strongest chance to raise that score in third grade?").

In addition to agreeing to the above approaches to talk about grouping and tracking, the faculty has been asked to evaluate this draft of this section of the school code on language ethics:

> As educators, we acknowledge that identification of groups or tracks
> poses the dangers of low expectation, altered school climate, and failure
> to observe or capitalize on the positive growth of students. Therefore,
> we maintain as a general ethical principle our determination to avoid
> any routine reference to children or classes solely in terms of their
> group or track designation. If their classified track or group assignment
> must be discussed for purposes of curriculum planning, we still seek to
> maintain a predominant tone of inquiry that reflects our belief that ev-
> ery child can make significant progress during every school year and
> that some children grow into or out of specific designations in the pro-
> cess of education.

Respect for Confidentiality in School Language

Privacy and confidentiality are the third key issue in the construction of a refocused school language environment. As discussed in the section on overall language environment, educators share the access of other professions (such as law or medicine) to confidential information about clients (students in this case). This may not have been as true in the past as it is today, when a great deal of information about children and families has become available to teachers through cumulative records, guidance counselors or social workers, school psychologists, and the increased use of technology to gain and share information. Some children may receive services in private psychiatric clinics, support groups connected to addiction or bereavement services, juvenile detention centers, or other social agencies that share information with schools.

In addition to the availability of school-based information, a great deal of casual disclosure is often available as well. In a media climate of full disclosure of intimate details about private lives, many more individuals may feel comfortable sharing confidential information about themselves and others to teachers. Likewise, children might talk with their teachers about questionable behavior of parents, chemical-dependence problems of family members, gang membership of brothers and sisters, or other possibly detrimental aspects of their lives at home. Faculty members who live in the community, parent and business volunteers, paraprofessionals, special support staff, and many others may have access to private information about children and their families.

The increased availability of confidential and personal information will make it necessary for the school code of language ethics to establish clear lines in two areas: (1) the difference between the compelling need to share information and the compelling ethical obligation to maintain confidence, and (2) the kinds of information that can be shared routinely and the kinds of information that must be held in strict confidence. It is often difficult to discern the appropriate ethical approach to specific areas of confidentiality. Two questions often can guide careful professional decisions: (1) Why does this person need to know? (2) Will the result of my disclosure of this information be beneficial or detrimental to the child and family?

An Ethical Approach to Confidentiality. This section will pose a problem that demonstrates the delicate balance that must be achieved while acting responsibly in issues of student privacy. Following a brief description of the situation, several questions will be posed for consideration.

Sheila's grades and standardized test scores have dropped in the past 2 years, and her behavior in school has become increasingly aggressive toward teachers and other students. The guidance counselor, who has conferred with the teachers, has called Sheila's home twice. Her mother has been withdrawn and uncommunicative during the conversations. Today, however, Sheila's mother came in to school to speak with her teacher, Mrs. Cookson. She wept during the meeting and confided that Sheila was moving at the end of the year to live with her aunt in a nearby community. It seems that Sheila recently had revealed to her minister that her older brother had been abusing her sexually for some time. The minister had called the state childline to make a formal child abuse report and also had spoken with Sheila's family. Reluctance to press criminal charges and inability to pay for private family therapy had contributed to the decision to send Sheila to live with another family for the time being.

Mrs. Cookson tried hard during the conversation to think about her ethical obligations in terms of confidentiality. She asked Sheila's mother at the end of the meeting if she had her permission to speak with the guidance counselor about the situation. At first reluctant, the mother did agree as long as she had the assurance that nothing would be written on Sheila's permanent record. Mrs. Cookson expressed warm regards to Sheila's mother and expressed hope that everything would turn out well for Sheila and her family.

Who needs to know about Sheila's situation, what do they need to know, and why? Mrs. Cookson correctly realized that the guidance counselor should know, because she was in the best position to help Sheila or support the family during this difficult transition. The emergent confidential information could help the guidance counselor to communicate with the family and to better interpret reports of difficulty from other teachers. Beyond discussion with the guidance counselor, however, Mrs. Cookson felt that she should keep this information in complete confidence.

Imagine, however, that another teacher in the school lives near Sheila's aunt and hears during a casual neighborhood conversation that Sheila has "really big problems." If this teacher approaches Mrs. Cookson to inquire, the appropriate answer could be, "Some problems of a confidential nature have come to my attention. While I cannot discuss them with you, I will say that I care very much about Sheila and want to help her and support her. It would be helpful if you would not repeat any information you have heard." If the other teacher actually had learned of the sexual abuse, and mentioned it directly to Mrs. Cookson, the response might be, "In the interest of professional confidentiality, I cannot discuss this with you. I would like to suggest, however, that we both protect and help Sheila by agreeing not to repeat this information to anyone else."

Now imagine that the gym teacher approaches Mrs. Cookson to share some concerns about Sheila's behavior. The appropriate response could be, "I will say that I am aware of some very sensitive and confidential issues affecting Sheila's family right now. You could mention her behavior to the guidance counselor, who is aware of the details of the problem. I want to help Sheila, and I really appreciate your kindness and continuing concern toward her. It could mean a great deal at this time."

Sheila's hypothetical situation opens up the complexity of the problem of confidentiality in schools. Mrs. Cookson made the decision to share information with the person most able to help Sheila and absolutely avoided any casual or irresponsible disclosure. Her continued responsibility would be to help Sheila as much as possible, to withhold potentially damaging information, and to acknowledge her knowledge of stress in Sheila's life when necessary.

"But wait," a concerned educator might say. "Why shouldn't all teachers be trusted to act in an ethical and professional manner? Shouldn't everyone who has contact with Sheila in the school know about her problems in order to help her?" Such questions underscore the critical importance of a carefully constructed code of language ethics in schools. While some problems (such as the sudden death of a parent) will be commonly known, other information is highly sensitive and its private nature deserves professional respect. Educators know well that not every colleague can be trusted to handle confidential information with compassion and secrecy. The best approach, in the interest of vulnerable students, is to create a protective ethical shield around information that could hurt even more deeply if handled improperly.

Even when the entire faculty does have access to information about a problem (perhaps the arrest of a parent reported as a scandal in the local newspaper), casual discussion should be avoided within the school. If just a few teachers know about a particular situation, they can share their knowledge of the need of the child for special understanding, without full disclosure of the problem. While the ideal is to trust all colleagues and administrators, the potential harm done by even one professional who engages in casual and unnecessary disclosure provides a rationale for a strong code of ethics to protect confidential information about students and families.

The Complexity of Confidentiality. The development of a school language code that effectively deals with the issue of confidentiality will be complex. Many other professions also are attempting to balance the ethics of confidentiality with the rapid expansion of technological information and the ever-increasing number of people who have access to private information about others. In an article on medical confidentiality, for example, Dr. Francis Collings stated, "Our medical records situation today is a joke! . . . one hundred people can look at an individual's records" (Shea, 1997, p. 34). Children must continue to depend on the efforts of educators to do their very best to protect the children's vulnerable private lives from inappropriate public scrutiny.

Protection of confidentiality in a school code of ethics implies trust and security in the private sharing of information and the existence of procedures to guarantee that information gathered about a child in the process of evaluation is kept private. Protection further implies that information that must be divulged will be kept to a minimum and that written records that become out of date or that potentially may be misused by others should be destroyed.

If protection of confidentiality is to be a strong and enduring principle of educational institutions, it will need to be a fully established component of the orientation of all new faculty members. In addition, there will need to be periodic review and discussion by faculty and others as to the nature of information received from and about people, and frequent consideration of the obligation assumed by all in the institution in guarding against misuses of that information (Ad Hoc Committee on Confidentiality of the National Social Welfare Assembly, 1958).

EXAMPLE OF A SCHOOL CONSIDERING
ISSUES OF CONFIDENTIALITY

The teachers and administrators of the Woodwell School have turned their attention to the issues of confidentiality within their school language environment. Because of the complexity of the issues, several smaller committees were formed to examine specific problems within the area of confidentiality. During subsequent discussion the total faculty identified the special importance of three types of information:

1. Information of a private nature that frequently is shared by parents, either about their own children or other children in their communities. The potential loss of confidentiality is greater because of the successful parent involvement program in the school.
2. Information that becomes available when children are referred for psychological evaluation and/or special services.
3. Information that becomes available when families are referred to the Friday support group run by the guidance counselor for parents whose children are experiencingproblems with school behavior.

In addition to identifying the key areas of confidentiality, the faculty has been asked to evaluate the draft of this section of the school code on language ethics:

> As educators, we acknowledge our constant exposure to confidential information about our students and their families. As a general principle, we maintain as confidential all private and potentially sensitive information unless, in sharing it with another professional, we are protecting or supporting the needs of a student. In addition, we recognize three specific areas of confidentiality within our school, which should be addressed: (1) private information shared by parents or discovered in conversation during parent volunteer activities, (2) information that becomes available during psychological testing and referral for special services, and (3) information that becomes available when families of children who have behavioral difficulties are referred to the Friday counselor support group. To counteract any problems created by access

to confidential information, all administrators, teachers, staff members, and volunteers in our building are required to attend a yearly meeting about the ethics of treatment of private information. In addition, all school personnel sign an annual school contract of commitment to maintain confidentiality of information gained in the process of providing human services to children and families.

CONCLUSION

Once a code of ethics has been developed for a specific school, decisions must be made about its dissemination and use. All who work in the school need to become familiar with the code, and it should be discussed on a yearly basis. In addition, a policy should be developed for the method by which the annual statement of confidentiality will be signed by administrators, teachers, support personnel, student teachers, school volunteers, and all others who will come into contact with information about students and families. Hopefully, the statement of ethics in language will support a renewed enthusiasm for the democratic goals of education throughout the school.

The following demonstrates how the hypothetical Woodwell School faculty might have refined their drafts into a formal code of ethics. It is provided so that other faculties embarking on the preparation of a similar language code have an example of a final outcome.

SAMPLE CODE OF ETHICS IN THE USE OF LANGUAGE IN SCHOOL

The entire faculty of the Woodwell School have a commitment to the ongoing development of a positive school language environment that supports excellence in teaching and the highest possible quality of service to all students. We believe that professional language is a behavior with serious repercussions for all connected to our school. Therefore, we have undertaken the development of this code of ethics to guide the ways in which we speak in every aspect of the provision of education to our students.

As educators, we acknowledge the existence of problems in the lives of students and families, and barriers both in social institutions and in social and political environments to the optimal development of our students. Yet, we seek to implement a school language characterized by the expectation of student success and the expectation of our own professional efficacy. We also seek a school language that differs from ordinary social language because, within our professional environment, all language should be geared toward protection of the well-being of students. We strongly discourage any professional language that denigrates either the present abilities or future potential of students, and stand firmly against language of prejudice and discrimination.

Goal 1. Any professional, parent, or visitor who enters our school will observe a language environment characterized by respect for our students, recognition of our students' potential, and hopeful expectation for our students' futures.

Goal 2. Any professional, parent, or visitor who enters our school will observe a language environment characterized by a tone of efficacy on the part of teachers and administrators who believe in their own power to successfully teach all students.

LANGUAGE AND DEFICIT TERMINOLOGY

As educators, we acknowledge the potential harm of deficit terminology applied to children. We seek a school language characterized by terms and descriptions that respect our students as capable individuals. Thus, we seek to eliminate from our school language whenever possible all terminology with the potential to lower expectations for students. In cases where terminology that applies to specific disorders/disabilities/program designations must be used, we seek to limit its use to areas of absolute necessity and also to apply the ethics of confidentiality at all times. A label or term is used only when connected to a positive intervention. Finally, we seek to avoid any global terminology that leads to generalizations and also to avoid labels that are not directly tied to positive intervention.

Goal 3. We seek to avoid any terminology that implies deficit or disability in our school.

Goal 4. We avoid any terms such as "at risk" or "dysfunctional family" that can create unfair and biased generalizations about students.

Goal 5. If terms/labels/designations must be used for purposes of positive intervention or funding, the ethics of confidentiality will be fully employed.

LANGUAGE ABOUT GROUPING AND TRACKING

As educators, we recognize the policy of our district to engage in limited tracking and ability grouping on all grade levels. We also acknowledge that the identification of groups or tracks poses the danger of lowering teacher expectations, creating a negative school climate, or limiting our sense of inquiry about the full potential of all students. Therefore, we maintain as a general principle the avoidance of any reference to children or classes in terms of their track or ability group as a regular part of our school language. When tracks or groups are discussed, for purposes of curriculum planning, we seek to maintain a tone of inquiry that assumes that all children have the potential to change and grow during the process of schooling.

> *Goal 6.* All teachers, administrators, and staff members will refer to children by room number, teacher, or period rather than track or ability group.
>
> *Goal 7.* Ability groups will be identified and discussed as such only in the course of scheduling or relevant curriculum planning.
>
> *Goal 8.* When abilities of groups or individuals are discussed, a tone of inquiry that implies the constant possibility of change or growth will characterize the discussion.

LANGUAGE ABOUT CONFIDENTIAL INFORMATION

As educators, we acknowledge our constant exposure to confidential information about our students and their families. As a general principle, we maintain as confidential all private and sensitive information unless, in sharing it with another appropriate professional, we clearly are protecting or supporting the needs of a student. In addition, we recognize four areas of confidentiality within our school, which must be addressed:

1. Private information shared by parents
2. Information made available through psychological testing and referral
3. Information made available through referral of families to a guidance support group because children are experiencing difficulties with behavior
4. Private information that becomes available from other sources such as parent or community volunteers

We constantly seek to make sensitive professional decisions about the need to share confidential information, and do so only when the process will strengthen the educational environment or provide greater protection for students. We avoid all casual conversation about sensitive information and seek to respect the privacy of our students and families as much as possible. A yearly meeting for teachers, administrators, staff members, and volunteers will be held to stress the importance of confidentiality, and a contract of confidentiality will be signed by all in the school who have access to information about students and families.

Goal 9. All private and confidential information about students is protected to the greatest possible extent.

Goal 10. The sharing of sensitive information is connected as closely as possible to the educational well-being and protection of the needs of students.

Goal 11. All teachers, administrators, staff members, and volunteers attend a yearly meeting about confidentiality and each year sign the following contract to maintain confidential information.

CONTRACT OF CONFIDENTIALITY

As teachers, administrators, staff members, visiting professionals, student teachers, and volunteers in the Woodwell School, we are united in our commitment to the protection of the privacy of students and families. We therefore recognize that all available information concerning test scores, ability groups or tracks, and problems in personal lives must be maintained in complete confidence. To that end, we agree to share confidential information only when absolutely necessary to provide supportive services for students. If parents share information with us in confidence, we agree to ask for the parents' permission to make further disclosure only to appropriate personnel. No information that becomes available to us within this school will be discussed in a casual manner or repeated outside the school.

I have read this statement, and I agree to uphold the principles of confidentiality therein. (Signed)

COMMITMENT TO ONGOING REFOCUS OF EDUCATIONAL LANGUAGE

As educators, we acknowledge our ongoing responsibility for construction of a total school environment that is likely to produce a professional language of sensitivity, inquiry, and efficacy. Our goal is always the creation of a school-language environment that provides the strongest possible foundation for excellence in education and equity in the provision of access to the very best this school has to offer to each and every one of our students.

References

Ad Hoc Committee on Confidentiality of the National Social Welfare Assembly. (1958). *Confidentiality in social services to individuals.* New York: National Social Welfare Assembly.

Airaksinen, T. (1993). Service and science in professional life. In R. F. Chadwick (Ed.), *Ethics and the professions* (pp. 1–26). Brookfield, VT: Avebury.

Applebome, P. (1997, January 12). School as America's cure-all. *New York Times,* Section 4, p. 4.

Archambault, R. D. (1964). *John Dewey on education: Selected writings.* New York: Random House.

Astuto, T. A., Clark, D. L., Read, A., McGree, K., & Fernandez, L. P. (1994). *Roots of reform: Challenging the assumptions that control change in education.* Bloomington, IN: Phi Delta Kappa.

Austin, J. L. (1962). *How to do things with words.* Oxford: Oxford University Press.

Banks, J. A. (1995a). The historical reconstruction of knowledge about race: Implications for transformative teaching. *Educational Researcher, 24*(2), 15–25.

Banks, J. A. (1995b). Multicultural education: Historical development, dimensions and practice. In J. A. Banks & C. A. McGee Banks (Eds.), *Handbook of research in multicultural education* (pp. 3–24). New York: Macmillan.

Baratz, S. S., & Baratz, J. C. (1970). Early childhood intervention: The social science base of institutional racism. *Harvard Educational Review, 40*(1), 29–50.

Bastian, A., Fruchter, N., Gittell, M., Greer, C., & Haskins, K. (1985). *Choosing equality: The case for democratic schooling.* Philadelphia: Temple University Press.

Bernard, B. (1993). Fostering resiliency in kids. *Educational Leadership, 51*(3), 44–48.

Berube, M. R. (1994). *American school reform: Progressive, equity, and excellence movements 1883–1993.* Westport, CT: Praeger.

Bourdieu, P. (1991). *Language and symbolic power* (J. B. Thompson, Ed.; G. Raymond & M. Adamson, Trans.). Cambridge, MA: Harvard University Press.

Brantlinger, E. A. (1993). *The politics of social class in secondary school.* New York: Teachers College Press.

Brown et al. v. Board of Education of Topeka, Sharnee County, Kansas et al., and Companion Cases, 74 Sup. Ct. 686 (1954).

Bruner, J. S. (1966). *Toward a theory of instruction.* New York: Norton.

Burrup, P. W., Brimley, V., & Garfield, D. R. (1988). *Financing education in a climate of change.* Boston: Allyn & Bacon.

Caws, P. (1996). *Ethics from experience.* Boston: Jones & Bartlett.

Chazan, M. (1973). The concept of compensatory education. In M. Chazan (Ed.), *Compensatory education* (pp. 1–26). London: Butterworths.

Checkley, K. (1996). The new union. Helping teachers take a lead in education reform. *Education Update, 38*(5), 1, 3–4, 8.

Children's Defense Fund. (1995). *The state of America's children.* Washington, DC: Author.

Cochran-Smith, M. (1995). Color blindness and basket wearing are not the answers: Confronting the dilemmas of race, culture and language diversity in teacher education. *American Educational Research Journal, 32*(3), 493–522.

Coleman, M., & Churchill, S. (1997). Challenges to family involvement. *Childhood Education, 73*(3), 144–148.

Conway, J. (1992). Three cheers for equality: The right name for diversity. *Educational Researcher, 21*(3), 29–30.

Cookson, P. W. (1995). Goals 2000: Framework for the new educational federalism. *Teachers College Record, 96*(3), 405–431.

Corbett, H. D., & Wilson, B. L. (1991). *Testing, reform, and rebellion.* Norwood, NJ: Ablex..

Crowe, L. D., Murray, W. I., & Smythe, H. A. (1966). *Educating the culturally disadvantaged child: Principles and programs.* New York: David McKay.

Cuffaro, H. K. (1995). *Experimenting with the world: John Dewey and the early childhood classroom.* New York: Teachers College Press.

Derman-Sparks, L. (1989). *Anti-bias curriculum: Tools for empowering young children.* Washington, DC: National Association for the Education of Young Children.

Deutsch, M., & Brown, B. R. (1967). Social influences in Negro–white intelligence differences. In Deutsch and Associates (Eds.), *The disadvantaged child: Selected papers of Martin Deutsch and Associates* (pp. 295–307). New York: Basic Books.

Edmonds, R. (1979). Effective schools for the urban poor. *Educational Leadership, 31*(1), 15–23.

Elkind, D. (1997). Schooling and family in the postmodern world. In A. Hargreaves (Ed.), *Rethinking educational change with heart and mind* (ASCD Yearbook, pp. 27–42). Alexandria, VA: Association for Supervision and Curriculum Development.

Ellis, A. K., & Fouts, J. T. (1994). *Research on school restructuring.* Princeton, NJ: Eye on Education.

Elmore, R. F. (1990a). Conclusion: Toward a transformation of public schooling. In R. F. Elmore & Associates (Eds.), *Restructuring schools: The next generation of educational reform* (pp. 267–284). San Francisco: Jossey-Bass.

Elmore, R. F. (1990b). Introduction: On changing the structure of public schools. In R. F. Elmore & Associates (Eds.), *Restructuring schools: The next generation of educational reform* (pp. 1–28). San Francisco: Jossey-Bass.

Elmore, R. F., & Furhman, S. H. (1995). Opportunity to learn standards and the state role in education. *Teachers College Record, 96*(3), 432–457.

Fehrenbacher, D. (1989). *Speeches and writings* (Vol. 1). New York: Library of America.

Fennimore, B. S. (1989). *Child advocacy for early childhood educators.* New York: Teachers College Press.

Fennimore, B. S. (1994). Addressing prejudiced statements: A four-step method that works. *Childhood Education, 70*(3), 202–203.

Fennimore, B. S. (1995). *Student-centered classroom management.* Albany, NY: Delmar.

Fennimore, B. S. (1996). Equity is not an option in public education. *Educational Leadership, 54*(2), 53–55.

Fine, M. (1993). Making controversy: Who's "at risk"? In R. Wollons (Ed.), *Children at risk in America: History, concepts and public policy* (pp. 91–110). Albany: State University of New York Press.

Finn, C. E. (1992). Introduction. In C .E. Finn & I. Rebarber (Eds.), *Education reform in the 90s* (pp. xi–xix). New York: Macmillan.

Fullan, M., & Hargreaves, A. (1996). *What's worth fighting for in your school?* New York: Teachers College Press.

Giroux, H. A. (1984). Rethinking the language of schooling. *Language Arts, 61*(1), 33–40.

Giroux, H. A. (1988a). *Schooling and the struggle for public life.* Minneapolis: University of Minnesota Press.

Giroux, H. A. (1988b). *Teachers as intellectuals: Toward a critical pedagogy of learning.* Granby, MA: Bergin & Garvey.

Giroux, H. A. (1992). Teachers as transformative intellectuals. In J. M. Rich (Ed.), *Innovations in education: Reformers and their critics* (pp. 67–102). Boston: Allyn & Bacon.

Glendon, M. A. (1991). *Rights talk: The impoverishment of political discourse.* New York: Free Press.

Goldberg, M. L. (1967). Methods and materials for educationally disadvantaged youth. In A. H. Passow, M. Goldberg, & A. J. Tannenbaum (Eds.), *Education of the disadvantaged: A book of readings* (pp. 369–398). New York: Holt, Rinehart and Winston.

Goldberg, M. L., Passow, A., & Justman, J. (1966). *The effects of ability grouping.* New York: Teachers College Press

Goleman, D. (1995). *Emotional intelligence.* New York: Bantam Books.

Good, T. L. (1996). Educational researchers comment on the education summit and other policy proclamations from 1983–1996. *Educational Researcher, 25*(8), 4–6.

Good, T. W., & Brophy, J. E. (1987). *Looking in classrooms* (4th ed.). New York: Harper & Row.

Goodlad, J. I. (1984). *A place called school.* New York: McGraw-Hill.

Goodlad, J. I. (1996). Democracy, education, and community. In R. Soder (Ed.), *Democracy, education, and the schools* (pp. 87–124). San Francisco: Jossey-Bass.

Gordon, E. W. (1968). Programs of compensatory education. In M. Deutsch, I. Katz, & A. R. Jensen (Eds.), *Social class, race, and psychological development* (pp. 381–410). New York: Holt, Rinehart and Winston.

Grant, C. A., & Tate, W. F. (1995). Multicultural education literature. In J. A. Banks & C. A. McGee Banks (Eds.), *Handbook of research in multicultural education* (pp. 145–166). New York: Macmillan.

Green, T. F. (1983). Excellence, equity and equality. In L. Schulman & G. Sykes (Eds.), *Handbook of teaching and policy* (pp. 318–341). New York: Longman.

Greene, M. (1973). *Teacher as stranger: Educational philosophy for the modern age.* Belmont, CA: Wadsworth.

Greene, M. (1985). The role of education in democracy. *Educational Horizons, 63,* 3–9.

Grumet, M. R. (1988). *Bitter milk: Women and teaching.* Amherst: University of Massachusetts Press.

Hamlin, R., Mukerji, R., & Yonemura, M. (1967). *Schools for young disadvantaged children.* New York: Teachers College Press.

Hansen, D. T. (1993). From role to person: The moral layeredness of classroom teaching. *American Educational Research Journal, 30*(4), 651–674.

Hargreaves, A. (1994). *Changing teachers, changing times. Teacher's work and culture in the postmodern age.* New York: Teachers College Press.

Hargreaves, A. (1997a). Introduction. In A. Hargreaves (Ed.), *Rethinking educational change with heart and mind* (1997 Yearbook, pp. vii–xxv). Alexandria, VA: Association for Supervision and Curriculum Development.

Hargreaves, A. (1997b). Rethinking educational change: Going deeper and wider in the quest for success. In A. Hargreaves (Ed.), *Rethinking educational change with heart and mind* (ASCD Yearbook, pp. 1–26). Alexandria, VA: Association for Supervision and Curriculum Development.

Heath, S. B., & Mangiola, L. (1991). *Children of promise: Literate activity in linguistically and culturally diverse classrooms.* Washington, DC: National Education Association.

Henry, C. (1993). Professional behavior and the organization. In R. F. Chadwick (Ed.), *Ethics and the professions* (pp. 145–155). Brookfield, VT: Avebury.

Herrnstein, R. J., & Murray, C. (1994). *The bell curve: Intelligence and class structure in American life.* New York: Free Press.

Heslep, R. D. (1989). *Education in democracy: Education's moral role in the democratic states.* Ames: Iowa State University Press.

Hilliard, A. G. (1976). The education of "inner-city" children. In R. C. Granger & J. C. Young (Eds.), *Demythologizing the inner-city child* (pp. 15–24). Washington, DC: National Association for the Education of Young Children.

Hoffman, D. M. (1996). Culture and self in multicultural education: Reflections on discourse, text and practice. *American Educational Research Journal, 33*(3), 545–569.

Holdsworth, D. (1993). Accountability: The obligation to lay oneself open to criticism. In R. F. Chadwick (Ed.), *Ethics and the professions* (pp. 42–57). Brookfield, VT: Avebury.

Hunt, J. M. (1968). Environment, development and scholastic achievement. In M. Deutsch, I. Katz, & A. R. Jensen (Eds.), *Social class, race and psychological development* (pp. 293–336). New York: Holt, Rinehart and Winston.

Irwin, J. R. (1973). *A ghetto principal speaks out.* Detroit: Wayne State University Press.

Jackson, J. (1993). Common codes: Divergent practices. In R. F. Chadwick (Ed.), *Ethics and the professions* (pp. 116–135). Brookfield, VT: Avebury.

Jensen, A. R. (1968). Social class and verbal learning. In M. Deutsch, I. Katz, & A. R. Jensen (Eds.), *Social class, race, and psychological development* (pp. 115–174). New York: Holt, Rinehart and Winston.

Jensen, A. R. (1969). How much can we boost IQ and scholastic achievement? *Harvard Educational Review*, 39(1), 1–123.

Jensen, A. R. (1973). *Educational differences*. London: Methuen.

Joyce, B., Wolf, J., & Calhoun, E. (1993). *The self renewing school*. Alexandria, VA: Association for Supervision and Curriculum Development.

Kerchner, C. T., & Mitchell, D. E. (1988). *The changing idea of a teacher's union*. New York: Falmer Press.

Kozol, J. (1967). *Death at an early age*. New York: Houghton Mifflin.

Kozol, J. (1990). *The night is dark and I am far from home*. New York: Simon & Schuster.

Kozol, J. (1991). *Savage inequalities: Children in America's schools*. New York: Harper Perennial.

Kultgen, J. (1988). *Ethics and professionalism*. Philadelphia: University of Pennsylvania Press.

Ladson-Billings, G. (1995). Multicultural teacher education: Research, practice and policy. In J. A. Banks & C. A. McGee Banks (Eds.), *Handbook of research in multicultural education* (pp. 747–762). New York: Macmillan.

MacKinnon, C. A. (1992). *Only words*. Cambridge, MA: Harvard University Press.

Mathews, D. (1996). *Is there a public for public schools?* Dayton, OH: Kettering Foundation Press.

Miller, R. (1990). *What are schools for? Holistic education in American culture*. Brandon, VT: Holistic Education Press.

Mitchell, A. (1997, January 19). Speaking softly in the bully pulpit. *New York Times*, pp. 1, 5.

Molnar, A. (1997). Why school reform is not enough to mend our civil society. *Educational Leadership*, 54(5), 37–39.

Mungazi, D. A. (1995). *Where he stands: Albert Shanker of the American Federation of Teachers*. Westport, CT: Praeger.

National Coalition of Advocates for Students. (1991). *The good common school: Making the vision work for all children*. Boston: Author.

National Commission on Children. (1991). *Beyond rhetoric: A new American agenda for children and families*. Washington, DC: Author.

National Commission on Teaching and America's Future. (1996). *What matters most: Teaching for America's future*. New York: Author.

National Education Association of the United States. (1964). *Opinions of the committee on professional ethics*. Washington, DC: Author.

Natriello, G. (1996). Diverting attention from conditions in American schools. *Educational Researcher*, 25(8), 7–9.

Natriello, G., McDill, E. L., & Pallas, A. M. (1990). *Schooling disadvantaged children: Racing against catastrophe*. New York: Teachers College Press.

Nieto, S. (1992). *Affirming diversity: The sociopolitical context of multicultural education*. New York: Longman.

Noblit, G. W. (1993). Power and caring. *American Educational Research Journal*, 30(1), 23–28.

Noddings, N. (1988). An ethic of caring and its implication for instructional arrangements. *American Journal of Education, 96*(2), 215–230.

Noddings, N. (1995). Caring. In V. Held (Ed.), *Justice and care: Essential readings in feminist ethics* (pp. 7–30). Boulder, CO: Westview Press.

Oakes, J. (1986). Tracking, inequality, and the rhetoric of school reform: Why schools didn't change. *Journal of Education, 168*(1), 60–80.

Oakes, J., Wells, A. S., Yonexawa, S., & Ray, K. (1997). Equity lessons from detracking schools. In A. Hargreaves (Ed.), *Rethinking educational change with heart and mind* (ASCD Yearbook, pp. 43–72). Alexandria, VA: Association for Supervision and Curriculum Development.

Ohanian, S. (1988). Huffing and puffing and blowing schools excellent. *Phi Delta Kappan, 66*(5), 316–321.

O'Neil, J. (1996). On emotional intelligence: A conversation with Daniel Goleman. *Educational Leadership, 54*(1), 6–11.

Orfield, G., & Eaton, S. E., & the Harvard Project on School Desegregation. (1996). *Dismantling desegregation: The quiet reversal of* Brown v. Board of Education. New York: New Press.

Page, R. N. (1991). *Lower track classrooms*. New York: Teachers College Press.

Parker, J. (1993). Moral philosophy—another "disabling profession"? In R. F. Chadwick (Ed.), *Ethics and the professions* (pp. 27–41). Brookfield, VT: Avebury.

Parker, W. C. (1996). Curriculum for democracy. In R. Soder (Ed.), *Democracy, education, and the schools* (pp. 182–210). San Francisco: Jossey-Bass.

Passow, A. H., & Elliott, D. L. (1968). The nature and needs of the educationally disadvantaged. In A. H. Passow (Ed.), *Developing programs for the educationally disadvantaged* (pp. 3–19). New York: Teachers College Press.

Peterson, P. E. (1983). *Background paper: Report of the Twentieth Century Fund Task Force on Federal Elementary and Secondary Policy*. New York: Twentieth Century Fund.

Placier, M. L. (1993). The semantics of state policy making: The case of "at risk." *Educational Evaluation and Policy Analysis, 15*(4), 380–395.

Polakow, V. (1993). *Lives on the edge: Single mothers and their children in the other America*. Chicago: University of Chicago Press.

Postman, N. (1966). *Language and reality*. New York: Holt, Rinehart and Winston.

Postman, N. (1979). *Teaching as a conserving activity*. New York: Delacorte Press.

Postman, N., & Weingartner, C. (1969). *Teaching as a subversive activity*. New York: Delacorte Press.

Putnam, H. (1994). *Words and life*. Cambridge, MA: Harvard University Press.

Raywid, M. A. (1990). Rethinking school governance. In R. F. Elmore & Associates (Eds.), *Restructuring schools: The next generation of educational reform* (pp. 152–205). San Francisco: Jossey-Bass.

Reinhart, J. R., & Lee, J. F., Jr. (1991). *American education and the dynamics of choice*. New York: Praeger.

Reissman, F. (1962). *The culturally deprived child*. New York: Harper & Brothers.

Rhees, R. (1963). Can there be a private language? In C. D. Caton (Ed.), *Philosophy and ordinary language* (pp. 90–107). Urbana: University of Illinois Press.

Rhyle, G. (1963). The theory of meaning. In C. E. Caton (Ed.), *Philosophy and ordinary language* (pp. 128–153). Urbana: University of Illinois Press.

Rist, R. C. (1970). Student social class and teacher expectations: The self-fulfilling prophecy in ghetto education. *Harvard Educational Review, 40*(3), 411–451.

Rist, R. C. (1973). *The urban school: A factory for failure.* Cambridge, MA: MIT Press.

Romanish, B. (1991). *Empowering teachers: Restructuring schools for the 21st century.* New York: University Press of America.

Sarason, S. B. (1990). *The predictable failure of school reform: Can we change course before it's too late?* San Francisco: Jossey-Bass.

Sarason, S. B. (1995). *Parental involvement and the political principle. Why the existing governance of schools should be abolished.* San Francisco: Jossey-Bass.

Sarason, S. B. (1996). *Revisiting "The culture of the school and the problem of change."* New York: Teachers College Press.

Scherer, M. (1996). On better alternatives for urban students: A conversation with Sylvia L. Peters. *Educational Leadership, 54*(2), 47–52.

Sergiovanni, T. J. (1992). *Moral leadership. Getting to the heart of school improvement.* San Francisco: Jossey-Bass.

Shea, J. (1997). Ethics for the orthodoxy. *Pennsylvania Gazette, 95*(7), 27–42.

Shulman, L. S. (1983). Autonomy and obligation: The remote control of teaching. In L. S. Shulman & G. Sykes (Eds.), *Handbook of teaching and policy* (pp. 484–504). New York: Longman.

Silin, J. G. (1995). *Sex, death, and the education of children: Our passion for ignorance in the age of AIDS.* New York: Teachers College Press.

Smith, F. (1990). *To think.* New York: Teachers College Press.

Smith, F. (1993). *Whose language? What power?: A universal conflict in a South African setting.* New York: Teachers College Press.

Smith, M. S., & Scoll, B. W. (1995). The Clinton human capital agenda. *Teachers College Record, 96*(3), 389–404.

Sockett, H. (1993). *The moral base for teacher professionalism.* New York: Teachers College Press.

Soder, R. (1996). Teaching the teachers of the people. In R. Soder (Ed.), *Democracy, education, and the schools* (pp. 244–274). San Francisco: Jossey-Bass.

Spring, J. (1976). *The sorting machine: National educational policy since 1945.* New York: David McKay.

Staten, H. (1984). *Wittengenstein and Derrida.* Lincoln: University of Nebraska Press.

Steinfels, P. (1992, December 27). Formative years. Seen, heard, and even worried about. *New York Times*, Section E, pp. 1, 12.

Stendler-Lavatelli, C. B. (1968). Environmental intervention in infancy and early childhood. In M. Deutsch, I. Katz, & A. R. Jensen (Eds.), *Social class, race, and psychological development* (pp. 347–380). New York: Holt, Rinehart and Winston.

Strawson, P. F. (1963). On referring. In C. E. Caton (Ed.), *Philosophy and ordinary language* (pp. 83–95). Urbana: University of Illinois Press.

Streshly, W. A., & De Mitchell, T. A. (1994). *Teacher unions and TOE: Building quality labor relations.* Thousand Oaks, CA: Corwin Press.

Strike, K. A., & Soltis, J. F. (1998). *The ethics of teaching*. New York: Teachers College Press.

Taylor, A. R. (1996). Conditions for American children, youth and families: Are we "world class"? *Educational Researcher, 25*(8), 10–12.

Thompson, J. B. (1991). Introduction. In P. Bourdieu, *Language and symbolic power* (J. B. Thompson, Ed.; G. Raymond & M. Adamson, Trans.) (pp. 1–31). Cambridge, MA: Harvard University Press.

Toulmin, S. E., & Baier, K. (1963). On describing. In C. E. Caton (Ed.), *Philosophy and ordinary language* (pp. 194–219). Urbana: University of Illinois Press.

Tyack, D. (1997). Civic education—What roles for citizens? *Educational Leadership, 54*(5), 22–24.

Tyack, D., & Cuban, L. (1995). *Tinkering toward utopia: A century of public school reform*. Cambridge, MA: Harvard University Press.

Valentine, C. A. (1971). Deficit, difference, and bicultural modes of Afro-American behavior. *Harvard Educational Review, 41*(2), 137–157.

Valli, L., Cooper, D., & Frankes, L. (1997). Professional development schools and equity. *Review of Research in Education, 22*, 251–304.

Weber, E. (1984). *Ideas influencing early childhood education: A theoretical analysis*. New York: Teachers College Press.

Weinberg, M. (1990). *Racism in the United States: A comprehensive classified bibliography*. New York: Greenwood Press.

Wesby-Gibson, D. (1969). *The disadvantaged child*. In D. L. Barclay (Ed.), *Art education for the disadvantaged child* (pp. 6–9). Washington, DC: National Art Education Association.

Willis, S. (1997). Parental rights: Proposed laws would affect parent–school relationships. *Education Update, 39*(1), 2–3.

Zeichner, K. M. (1992). *Educating teachers for cultural diversity* (Special Report). East Lansing, MI: National Center for Research on Teacher Learning.

Index

and democracy, 28
and ethics, 121, 132, 143–45, 153
and school reform, 64, 65
See also Classification
Transformational language, 17–18, 32–34, 35–36, 100
Transformative, teachers as, 31
Truth, 11, 14, 25
Tyack, D., 70, 92, 93

Unionism, 107–10, 137

Valentine, C.A., 83
Valli, L., 106
Violence, 3, 5, 6, 12, 16. *See also* Abuse
Vision
  as advocacy, 7–8
  and conceptualizing educational language environments, 10
  and democracy, 25
  and leadership, 91

and outside-in look at educational language, 4
and power of language, 10
and school reform, 59, 62
and talk about teachers, 46
and teacher education, 105
and unionism, 109

Weber, E., 86
Weinberg, M., 87
Weingartner, C., 1–2, 5, 17, 21, 86
Wesby-Gibson, D., 77
Westinghouse Learning Corporation, 82
Willa (example), 79–80
Willis, S., 73, 74
Wilson, B.L., 96
Woodwell Elementary School (example), 137–39, 141–45, 149–53

Zeichner, K.M., 31
Zero tolerance, 126-27, 128